embers

One Ojibway's Meditations

RICHARD WAGAMESE

Douglas & McIntyre

7 8 9 10 — 24 23 22 21 20 19 18

Douglas and McIntyre (2013) Ltd.
P.O. Box 219, Madeira Park, BC, V0N 2H0
www.douglas-mcintyre.com

Edited by Barbara Pulling
Cover design by Anna Comfort O'Keeffe
Text design by Diane Robertson

Printed and bound in Canada

Douglas and McIntyre (2013) Ltd. acknowledges the support of the Canada Council for the Arts, which last year invested $153 million to bring the arts to Canadians throughout the country. We also gratefully acknowledge financial support from the Government of Canada through the Canada Book Fund and from the Province of British Columbia through the BC Arts Council and the Book Publishing Tax Credit.

Library and Archives Canada Cataloguing in Publication

Wagamese, Richard, author
Embers : one Ojibway's meditations / Richard Wagamese

Issued in print and electronic formats.
ISBN 978-1-77162-133-5 (paperback).--ISBN 978-1-77162-134-2 (html)

1. Wagamese, Richard. 2. Ojibwa Indians--Religion. I. Title.
E99.C6W33 2016 299.7'8333 C2016-905524-8
C2016-905525-6

This book is dedicated to the memory of Jack Kakakaway, my spiritual father, who brought me fully into the world, and to Yvette Lehmann, who keeps me fully there in all possible ways.

Contents

Introduction

MORNINGS HAVE BECOME my table.

At dawn each day, I creep from my bedroom down the hall to the kitchen, where I set my tea to brew and then move to the living room to wait. In the immaculate silence, I watch the world unfurl from shadow. I listen to the sounds of birds, the wind along the eaves, the creak of floorboards and joists and rafters in this small house I call my home.

When the tea is ready, I cradle the cup in my palms and inhale the scent of lavender. I place the cup on the living room table. Then I rise to retrieve the bundle that holds the sacred articles of my ceremonial life. I open it and remove my smudging bowl, my eagle wing fan, my rattle and the four sacred medicines of my people—sage, sweet grass, tobacco and cedar. I put small pinches of each together in the smudging bowl, which I set upon the table. I close my eyes and breathe for a few moments. Then I light the medicines, using a wooden match, and waft the smoke around and over my head and heart and body with the eagle wing fan. When I am finished, I set the fan on the table, too.

There are certain spiritually oriented books I read from each morning. I lift the books from the couch beside me and read from them in turn. Then I place the books on the table as well. I close my eyes and consider what the readings have to tell me that day. When I'm ready, I settle deeper into the burgeoning pool of quietude, and when I feel calm and centred and at peace, I say a prayer of gratitude for all the blessings that are present in my life. I ask to be guided through the day with the memory of this sacred time, this prayer, the smell of these medicines in the air, and the peace and calm in my heart. I pick up the role Creator has asked me to play in this reality.

The small meditations in this book come from my early mornings at that living room table. Later, at the desk in my writing space, I write the meditations as they come to me, before turning to the writing that is my life and passion and career. A meditation doesn't come every morning. Sometimes one doesn't arrive for days. But when my connection to those things on the table has been strongest, when I have been joined to those things completely, the meditations rise unbidden and form themselves on the page almost as if I were taking dictation. I believe they have been conjured in me. Everything I have come to know and rely upon as centring, spiritual, real and valid has its place on that table in my living room. The table is like my life: dented, scarred, battered and worn, but rich and full nonetheless, and singing its histories. In that way, mornings themselves have become my table. Enveloped in Ojibway ceremony, protocol and ritual, ringed by strong words on faith, love, resilience, mindfulness and calm, I reclaim myself each morning. I walk out into the world in a position of balance, ready to do what Creator asks of me that day.

The words in this book are embers from the tribal fires that used to burn in our villages. They are embers from the spiritual fires burning in the hearts, minds and souls of great writers on healing and love. They are embers from every story I have ever heard. They are embers from all the relationships that have sustained and defined me. They are heart songs. They are spirit songs. And, shared with you, they become honour songs for the ritual ways that spawned them. Bring these words into your life. Feel them. Sit with them. Use them.

For this is the morning, excellent and fair...

I.

stillness

BLESSINGS
are in the
WIND

I AM MY silence. I am not the busyness of my thoughts or the daily rhythm of my actions. I am not the stuff that constitutes my world. I am not my talk. I am not my actions. I am my silence. I am the consciousness that perceives all these things. When I go to my consciousness, to that great pool of silence that observes the intricacies of my life, I am aware that I am me. I take a little time each day to sit in silence so that I can move outward in balance into the great clamour of living.

I AM A dreamer made real by virtue of the world touching me. This is what I know. I am spirit borne by a body that moves through the dream that is this living, and what it gathers to keep becomes me, shapes me, defines me. The dreamer I am is vivid when I fully inhabit myself—when I allow that. Meditation is not an isolated act of consciousness. It's connecting to the dream. It's being still so that the wonder of spirit can flow outward, so that the world touches me and I touch the world. It's leaving my body and my mind and becoming spirit again, whole and perfect and shining.

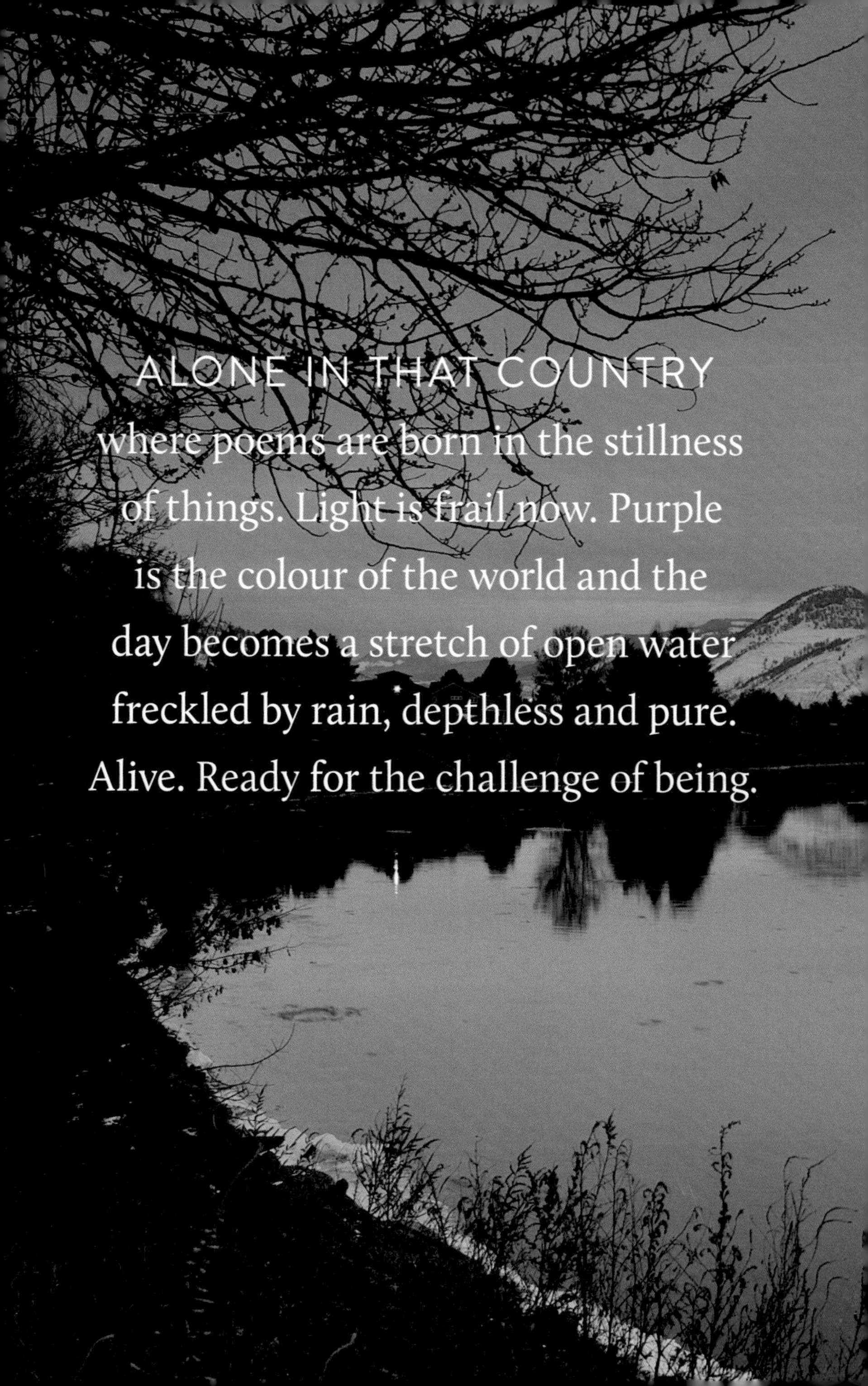

ALONE IN THAT COUNTRY
where poems are born in the stillness
of things. Light is frail now. Purple
is the colour of the world and the
day becomes a stretch of open water
freckled by rain, depthless and pure.
Alive. Ready for the challenge of being.

THERE IS SUCH A POWERFUL eloquence in silence. True genius is knowing when to say nothing, to allow the experience, the moment itself, to carry the message, to say what needs to be said. Words are less important, less effective than feeling. When you can sit in perfect silence with someone, you truly know how to communicate.

ME: What's the best way to learn to be spiritual?

OLD WOMAN: Pack light.

ME: What do you mean?

OLD WOMAN: Carry only what you need for the journey. Don't tire yourself out with unnecessary stuff.

ME: Like what?

OLD WOMAN: Like your head. Like your talk. Spirituality isn't found in your head. It's found in your heart. It isn't found in big, important-sounding words or long speeches. It's found in silence. If you travel with your heart and your quiet, you'll find the way to spiritual.

***

I found my first step on the journey that day.

AROUND ME DRIFTS the smoke of the medicines. This has become my favourite time, this hour just before dawn when the shapes of things reclaim their daylight boundaries and everything everywhere edges into wakefulness. My teachers say that all good things require sacrifice. Meeting this hour of prayerfulness and gratitude means I sacrifice the warmth of my bed. But the reward is inward stillness. In this waking world, I am awakened. In this easing of shadow, I reclaim the light. I am not alone here. I sit with my ancestors, singing this day into being—and I am made more.

SOMETIMES PEOPLE JUST need to talk. They need to be heard. They need the validation of my time, my silence, my unspoken compassion. They don't need advice, sympathy or counselling. They need to hear the sound of their own voices speaking their own truths, articulating their own feelings, as those may be at a particular moment. Then, when they're finished, they simply need a nod of the head, a pat on the shoulder or a hug. I'm learning that sometimes silence really is golden, and that sometimes "Fuck, eh?" is as spiritual a thing as needs to be said.

Nothing
IN THE
UNIVERSE
ever grew
FROM THE
outside IN.

I WANT TO listen deeply enough that I hear everything and nothing at the same time and am made more by the enduring quality of my silence. I want to question deeply enough that I am made more not by the answers so much as my desire to continue asking questions. I want to speak deeply enough that I am made more by the articulation of my truth shifting into the day's shape. In this way, listening, pondering and sharing become my connection to the oneness of life, and there is no longer any part of me in exile.

MY SPIRITUAL FATHER once told me, "Nothing in the universe ever grew from the outside in." I like that. It keeps me grounded. It reminds me to be less concerned with outside answers and more focused on the questions inside. It's the quest for those answers that will lead me to the highest possible version of myself.

IN THE BUSH, knee-deep in snow, laying tobacco down and offering prayers of thankfulness for the life of my mother, I became aware of silence. It was full and rich and tangible: I could almost reach out and touch it. I smiled then. Smiled because it becomes so simple when you surrender grief to the ongoing act of living, to being, to becoming. You become aware of the silences that exist between words, between actions, choices, results, changes. That's where you grow—in those silences. All that you feel is all that you are, and all that you know is all that you know, and you emerge from that silence ready to live out loud again: sore and blue and jubilant, outrageous and raucous and clamouring for more. The sound of silence. The sound of self emerging.

I AM CONSTANTLY surrounded by noise: TV, texts, the internet, music, meaningless small talk, my thinking. All of it blocks my consciousness, my ability to hear the ME that exists beneath the cacophony. I am my consciousness, my awareness of my circumstance, my presence in every moment. So I cultivate silence every morning. I sit in it, bask in it, wrap it around myself, and hear and feel me. Then, wherever the day takes me, the people I meet are the beneficiaries of my having taken that time—they get the real me, not someone shaped and altered by the noise around me. Silence is the stuff of life.

A WORLD SO still you swear you can hear her breathe. Snow glitters with points of light flung like stars across a universe of white. Not even birds breach the air, and there rises within you the notion that stillness is more enriching than motion, listening is more empowering than distraction and slow, measured steps feel more graceful than speed. Ah, I'm growing old, you say—then marvel at how young and new and invigorated it makes you feel.

I AM NOT created or re-created by the noise and clatter of my life, by the rush and scurry, the relentless chase or the presumption that more gets more. No, I am created and re-created by moments of stillness and quiet. I am struck richer by a pure solitude that allows me to feel the world around me and lean into my place in it. I am not the rush of words in my life's narrative. I am its punctuation. Its pauses and stops. I am my ongoing recharge; in this silence I am reborn.

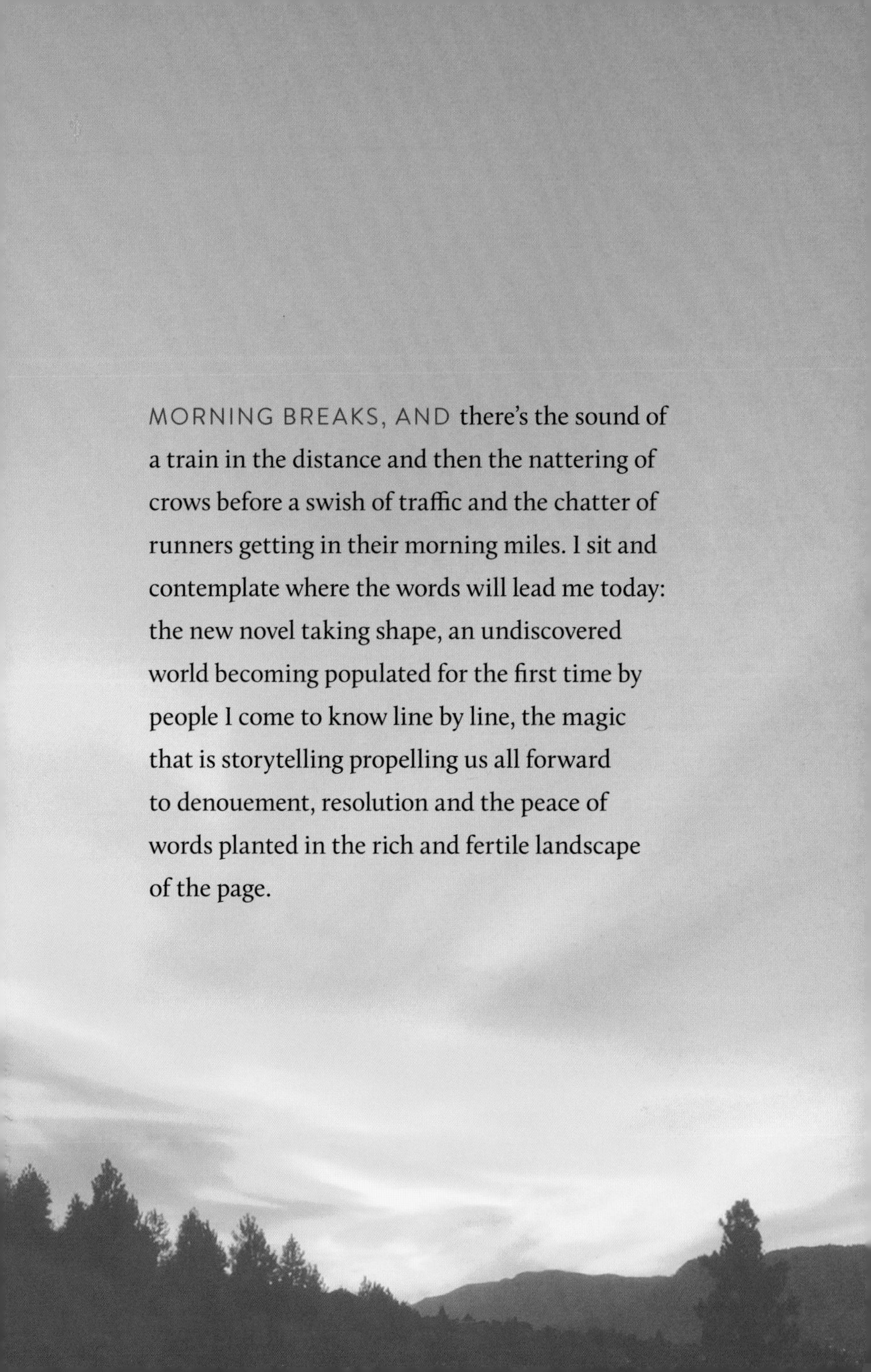

MORNING BREAKS, AND there's the sound of a train in the distance and then the nattering of crows before a swish of traffic and the chatter of runners getting in their morning miles. I sit and contemplate where the words will lead me today: the new novel taking shape, an undiscovered world becoming populated for the first time by people I come to know line by line, the magic that is storytelling propelling us all forward to denouement, resolution and the peace of words planted in the rich and fertile landscape of the page.

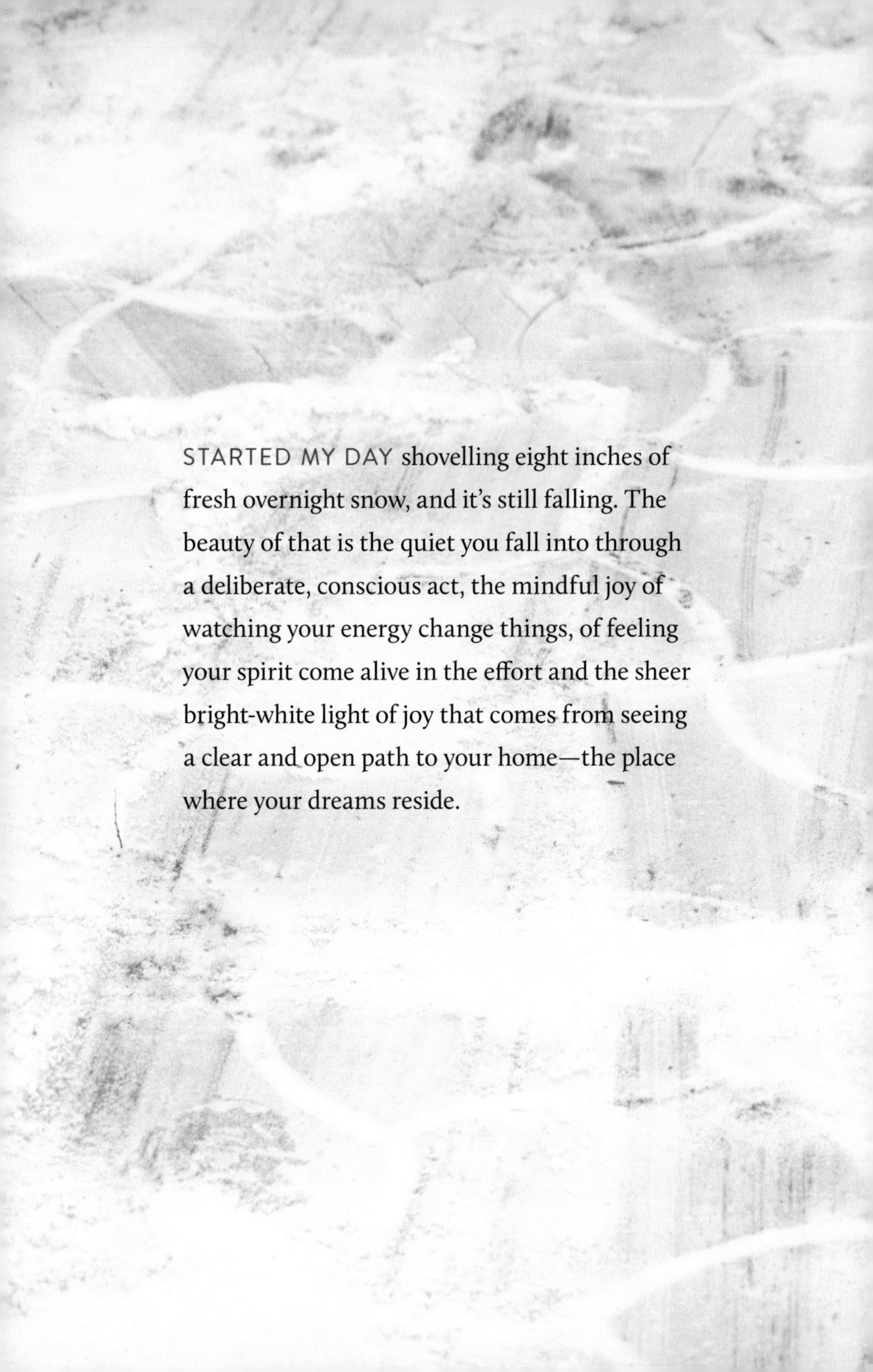

STARTED MY DAY shovelling eight inches of fresh overnight snow, and it's still falling. The beauty of that is the quiet you fall into through a deliberate, conscious act, the mindful joy of watching your energy change things, of feeling your spirit come alive in the effort and the sheer bright-white light of joy that comes from seeing a clear and open path to your home—the place where your dreams reside.

ME: What is the purpose of ceremony?

OLD WOMAN: To lead you to yourself.

ME: How?

OLD WOMAN: By giving you an idea of who you want to be and then allowing you to create the experience of being that way.

ME: Which ceremony is the best, then?

OLD WOMAN: Life. Choose what leads you to the highest vision you can have of yourself, and then choose what allows you to express that. What you express, you experience. What you experience, you are.

ME: How do I prepare?

OLD WOMAN: Breathe...

THERE ARE MOTIONS of the heart that occur only in quiet rooms, in the splendour of solitude where nothing and everything exists at the same time. Being and becoming have their confluence in these moments of touching your essence. You feel yourself a part of the great wheel of creative, nurturing, loving, benevolent energy that is spinning around us all the time. This is what it means to be spiritual—to feel your spirit moving. Take to quiet places, then. Immerse yourself in them. Feel your energy merge with that timeless, eternal energy and be made more.

IN THIS STILLNESS, I am the trees alive with singing. I am the sky everywhere at once. I am the snow and the wind bearing stories across geographies and generations. I am the light everywhere descending. I am my heart evoking drum song. I am my spirit rising. In the smell of these sacred medicines burning, I am my prayers and my meditation, and I am time captured fully in this now. I am a traveller on a sacred journey through this one shining day.

I AM A
traveller
ON A
sacred
journey
THROUGH THIS
one shining
day.

I DON'T KNOW the word for it, that space between seconds, but I've come to understand for myself that it's the punctuation of my life. Between each word, each thought, each moment is where the truth of things lies. The more intent I am on hearing it, seeing it, feeling it, incorporating it, the more precise the degree to which I'm focused on my life and the act of living. I want to dive into those small bits of silence. They contain the ocean of my being and our togetherness. So if I don't respond quickly, excuse me. I'm busy allowing the surf of consciousness to break over me so that I can stand on the coast of our unity and be more.

II.

harmony

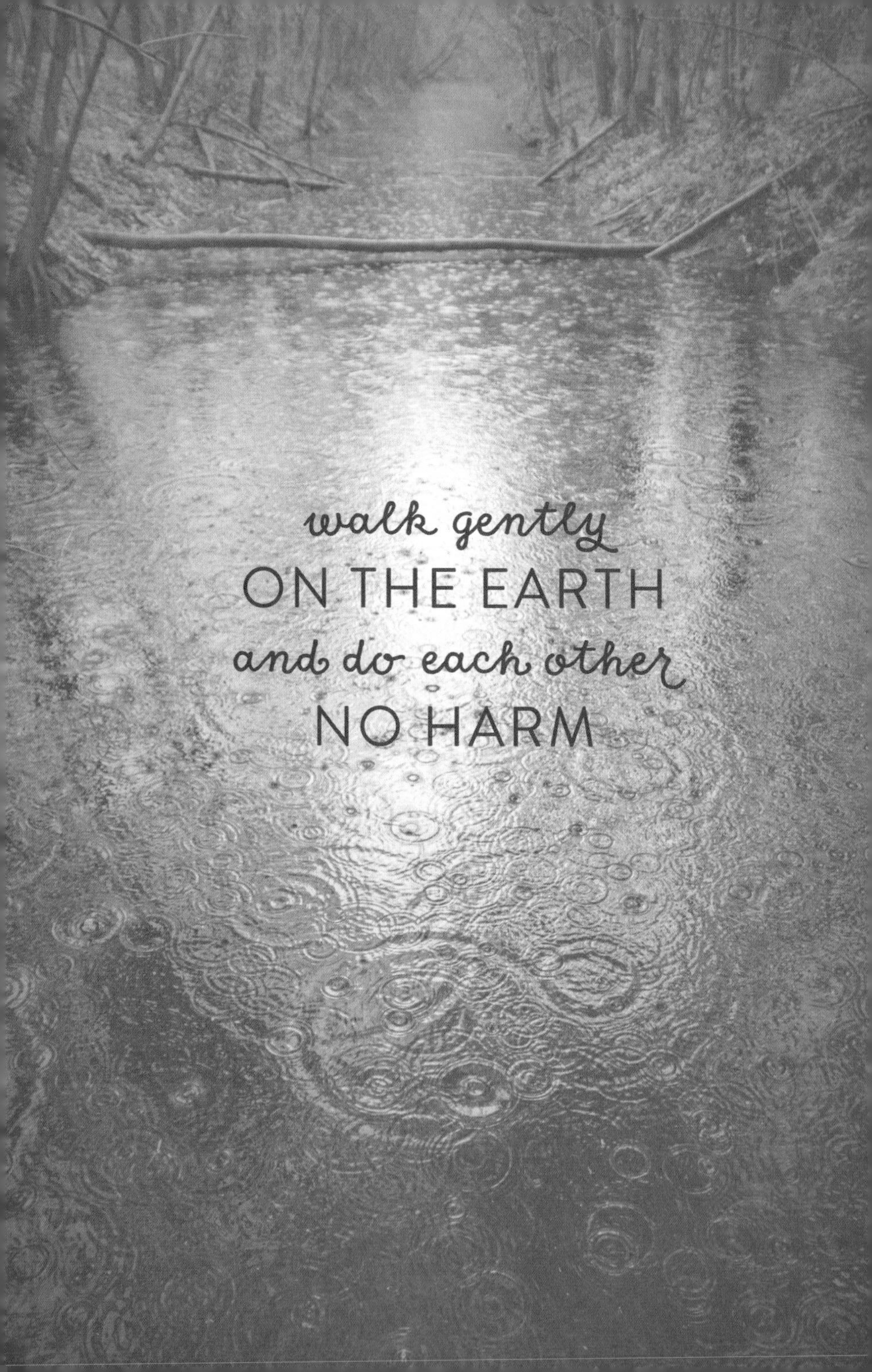
walk gently
ON THE EARTH
and do each other
NO HARM

FOG DRIFTS ACROSS the harbour the way a cat slinks across a room, and in that jaw-dropping silence are mystery and elegance and power. Sitting here on a morning grey as stone, in a city on an island tucked against a mountain, you come to realize how dynamic living on a planet can be when you remember that we're on one. This great island tucked against the bowl of space is home. It is majestic and at the same time a humble being—allowing us all to grow and evolve. Aki—Earth. I will walk her skin today attuned to her heartbeat, the feel of her thrumming against the soles of my feet.

I'VE BEEN CONSIDERING the phrase "all my relations" for some time now. It's hugely important. It's our saving grace in the end. It points to the truth that we are all related, that we are all connected, that we all belong to each other. The most important word is "all." Not just those who look like me, sing like me, dance like me, speak like me, pray like me or behave like me. ALL my relations. That means every person, just as it means every rock, mineral, blade of grass, and creature. We live because everything else does. If we were to choose collectively to live that teaching, the energy of our change of consciousness would heal each of us—and heal the planet.

We live because
EVERYTHING ELSE DOES.

WE APPROACH OUR lives on different trajectories, each of us spinning in our own separate, shining orbits. What gives this life its resonance is when those trajectories cross and we become engaged with each other, for as long or as fleetingly as we do. There's a shared energy then, and it can feel as though the whole universe is in the process of coming together. I live for those times. No one is truly ever "just passing through." Every encounter has within it the power of enchantment, if we're willing to look for it.

ONE WINDY DAY in summer many summers ago, a hawk hurtled straight down at me. Ten feet above my head, she spread her wings and stopped in mid-dive. I heard the whoosh of her wings against the sound of the wind and the exhalation of my own breath. Three things collided in an instant: wind, hawk, breath. There was no separation. We were connected. Joined by air. In the flash of that sacred moment, I understood what it is to be alive: to be connected, to be aware of that connection, to be grateful for it. To breathe is to take in the wind of all breath. To exhale slowly is to open myself and glide over everything I feel.

UNITY CANNOT EXIST when exclusion is allowed to occur. I was graced with this teaching years ago, when I was working as a traditional elder's helper. The teaching was given in the context of the sacred pipe, but its intention was to help me understand community. What brings us together cannot exist in the same time and place as what keeps us apart. You. Me. Everyone. My choice is to be aware of our similarities: our yearning for truth, peace, love, belonging, welcome, grace, mercy, a god of our own understanding and at least one moment of real contact at the heart of every day. Seeing that, I am made more, included, extended and in harmony...until that moment when I no longer see.

ME: Why am I alive?

OLD WOMAN: Because everything else is.

ME: No. I mean the purpose.

OLD WOMAN: That is the purpose. To learn about your relatives.

ME: My family?

OLD WOMAN: Yes. The moon, stars, rocks, trees, plants, water, insects, birds, mammals. Your whole family. Learn about that relationship. How you're moving through time and space together. That's why you're alive.

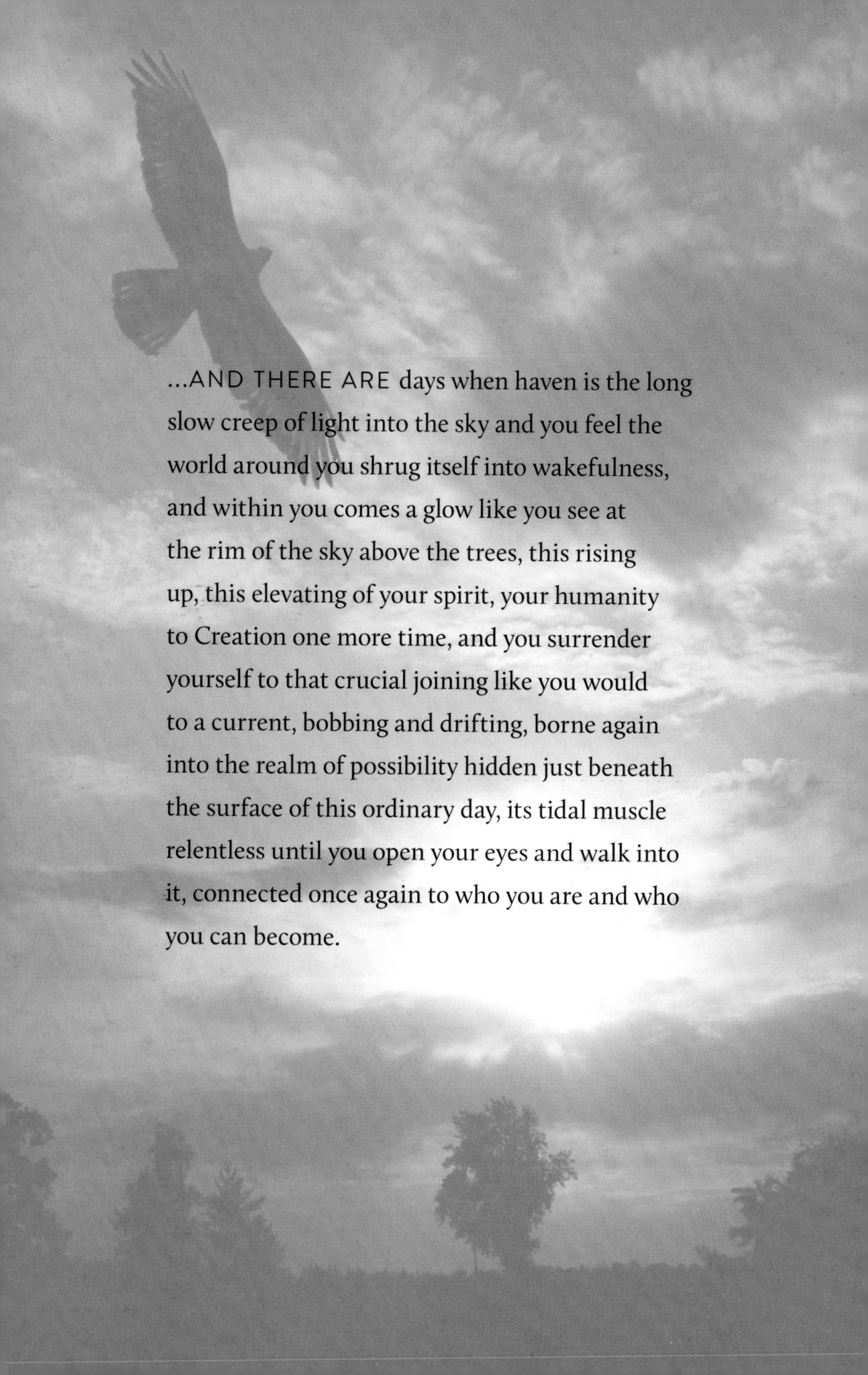

...AND THERE ARE days when haven is the long slow creep of light into the sky and you feel the world around you shrug itself into wakefulness, and within you comes a glow like you see at the rim of the sky above the trees, this rising up, this elevating of your spirit, your humanity to Creation one more time, and you surrender yourself to that crucial joining like you would to a current, bobbing and drifting, borne again into the realm of possibility hidden just beneath the surface of this ordinary day, its tidal muscle relentless until you open your eyes and walk into it, connected once again to who you are and who you can become.

LIKE MOST OF us do, I spent a lot of time trying to compress things into a context I could accept. That was hard work, and it meant I was alone most of the time. Nowadays, I figure life is pretty simple: Creator is everywhere and divine light shines through everything and everyone all the time. My work is to look for that light. In those fleeting, glorious instances when I see it, I am made more, right then, right there.

TODAY, ONCE AGAIN, I surrender my gift to Creator and ask that it be directed, channelled through me, every word, phrase, sentence guided by Her intention. Then I sit and write and watch the Great Mystery expelled upon the page. This marvellous gift has become my life by virtue of my always remembering where it comes from and claiming only the discipline, dedication, sacrifice and commitment as my own. All else is Creator's. If art is not spiritual, it suffers from our human limitations.

FROM OUR VERY first breath, we are in relationship. With that indrawn draft of air, we become joined to everything that ever was, is and ever will be. When we exhale, we forge that relationship by virtue of the act of living. Our breath commingles with all breath, and we are a part of everything. That's the simple fact of things. We are born into a state of relationship, and our ceremonies and rituals are guides to lead us deeper into that relationship with all things. Big lesson? Relationships never end; they just change. In believing that lies the freedom to carry compassion, empathy, love, kindness and respect into and through whatever changes. We are made more by that practice.

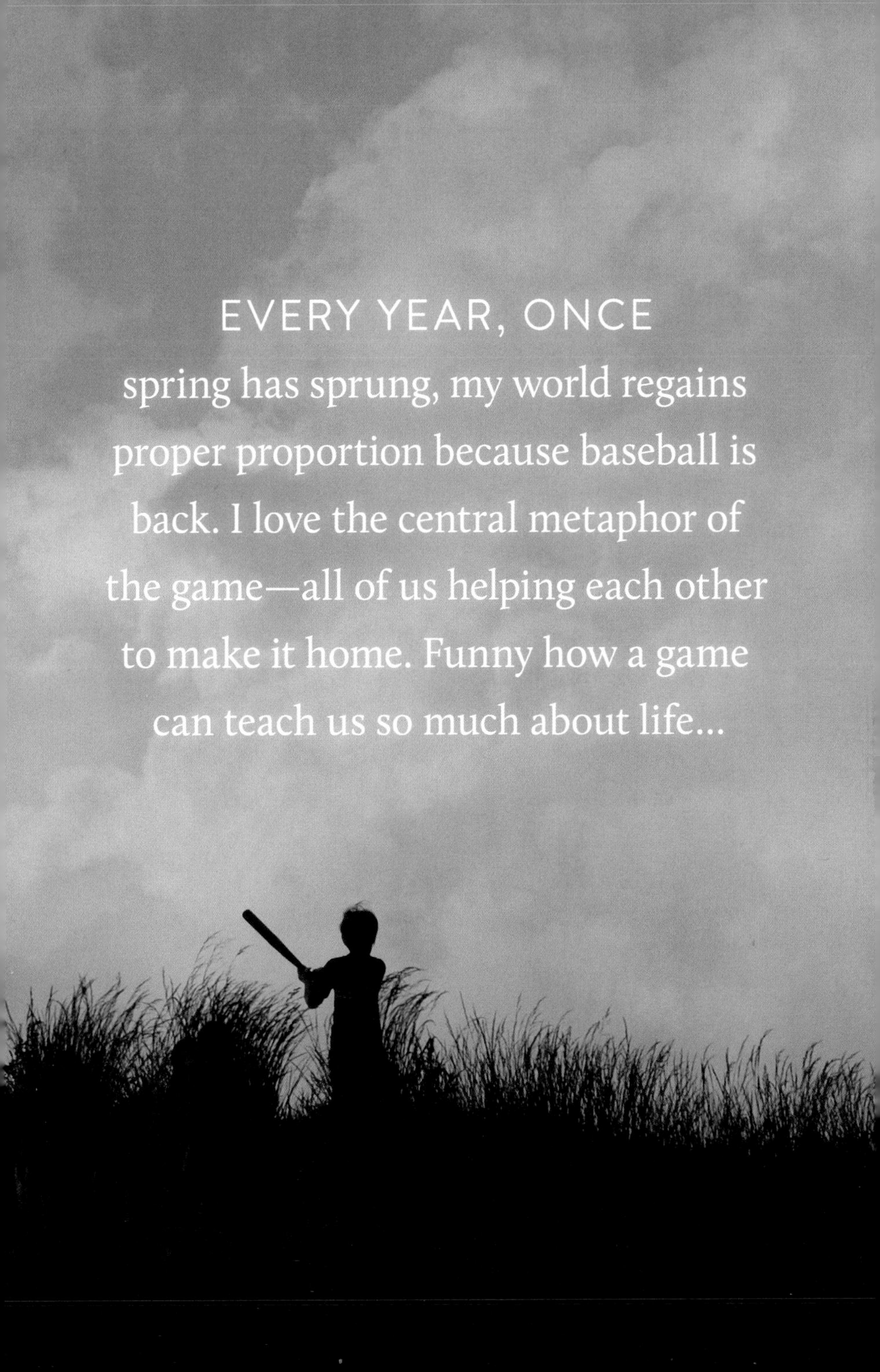

EVERY YEAR, ONCE spring has sprung, my world regains proper proportion because baseball is back. I love the central metaphor of the game—all of us helping each other to make it home. Funny how a game can teach us so much about life...

IT IS LOVE itself that brings us all together. This human family we are part of, this singular voice that is the accumulation of all voices raised together in praise of all Creation, this one heartbeat, this one drum, this one immaculate love that put us here together so that we could learn its primary teaching—that love is the energy of Creation, that it takes love to create love.

RETURNING IS A wonderful thing when great friends are involved. Years dissolve and time is irrelevant in the light of true reunion. It means to become one again. It means to be joined. It means to be one spirit, one energy, one song. It means to be returned to the balance you find when friendships are struck—and the entryway is a hug.

THREE STRANDS IN a braid of sweet grass. They represent three spiritual qualities—maybe love, kindness, humility. When I smudge myself, I purify myself in those qualities. I prepare myself for my day with the strength of those spiritual qualities. The smoke clings to my hair, my clothes, and it remains in the air of my home. As I move through the day and smell that fragrance, I am reminded of how I have chosen to live—and in that is the power of greeting each day with reverence, calm and prayer. That is how I learn to direct my humanity toward peace, equality and harmony: one day, one person, one circumstance at a time.

Tree talk,
TREE PEOPLE,
AS MY OWN
people say

THEY USED TO call me a nut. Back then, it was a putdown of my overwhelming curiosity. But I've learned nuts are formed from symbiotic relationships between trees. They communicate through fungal networks in the soil. In a process called mast seeding, different species of trees communicate and come into fruit (the delivery of nuts) at the same time, ensuring their ongoing survival. Tree talk, tree people, as my own people say. These days, I'm definitely a nut, learning to exist in unity, synchrony and harmony.

ON MY OWN in the country of my people, and I feel the lure and tug of the land as insistently as a lover's grasp. This is where poems are born, where stories are nurtured within me, and it is here, among the cliff and stone and bush and waters, where I am most fully the creation that I am. I stand solid here. I am the moose and bear and pickerel. I am tamarack, pine and lichen. I am the rich brown of the earth and the eternal bowl of the sky. Home. Where I am articulated and defined in the context of geography.

I USED TO believe my body contained my soul. That was fine for a while. But when I started thinking about oneness with Creator, I came to believe that it's the other way around. My soul contains my body. It is everything that I am. I am never separate from Creator except within my mind. That's the ultimate truth, and I need to be reminded, to learn again, to learn anew in order to get it. When I do, I know the truth of what my people say: that we are all spirit, we are all energy, joined to everything that is everywhere, all things coming true together.

WHEN THE MUSE is full upon you, you move to the chair at your desk as if entranced, and in that ghostly glow against the full dark before sunrise, story becomes a shape-shifter, a presence that cajoles you, tempts you, coaxes words to eke out onto the page, creating worlds and people from the fire deep within you so that this alchemy of creation becomes transcendent, making time lose all its properties. There is just you and the universe and this creative fire moving through your fingers in bold palettes of colour chasing the dark away until you emerge in the sure, calm light of morning and feel like a writer again.

OLD WOMAN: Always be a gentleman, my boy.

ME: You mean polite, gracious, humble?

OLD WOMAN: No, I mean always be a gentle man. Act softly and kindly to others and to yourself.

ME: In everything?

OLD WOMAN: Yes. In everything. You don't need to be hard, like others may say. Hard things break. Soft things never do. Be like grass. It gets stepped on and flattened but regains its shape again once the pressure passes. It is humble, accepting and soft. That's what makes it strong.

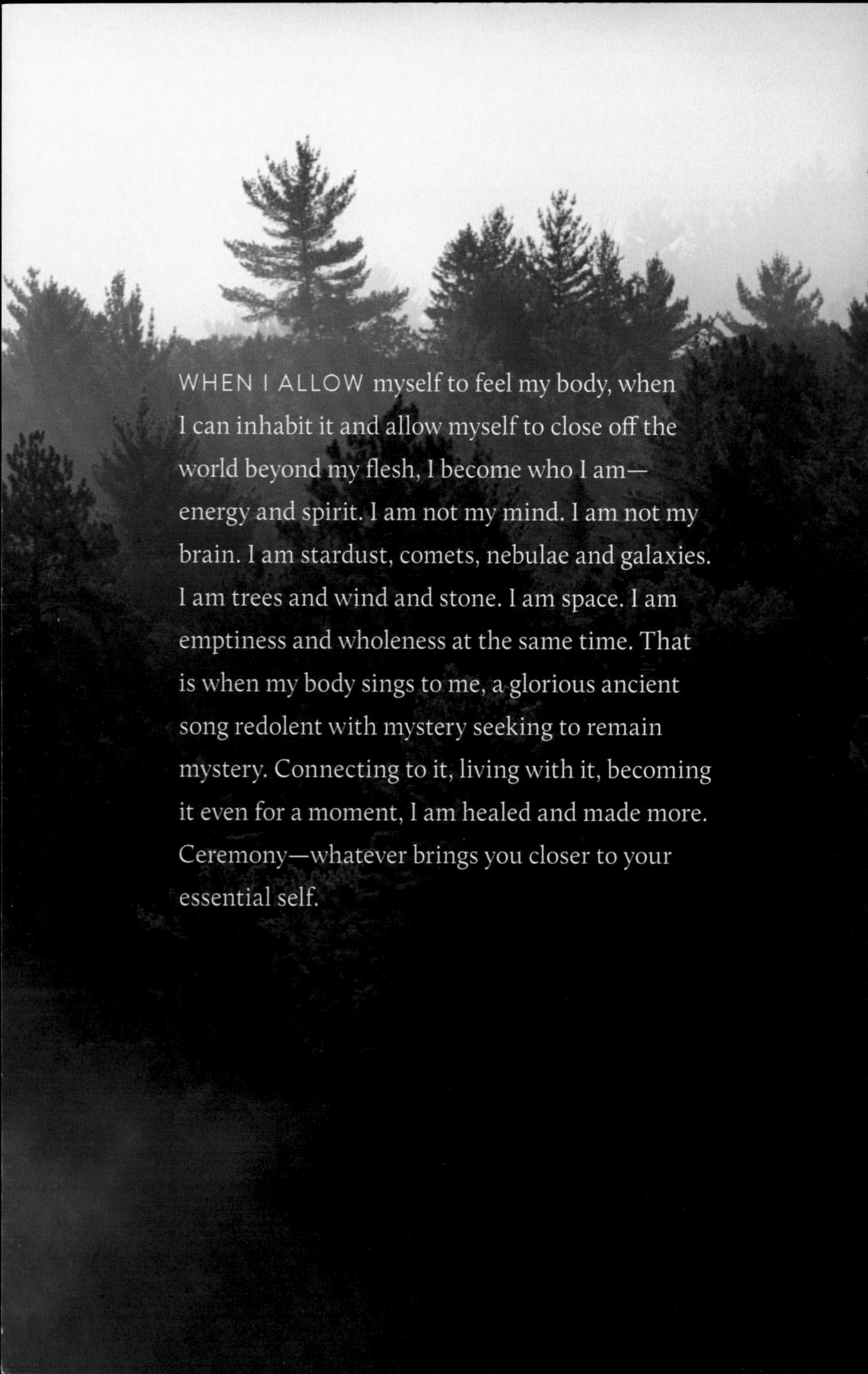

WHEN I ALLOW myself to feel my body, when I can inhabit it and allow myself to close off the world beyond my flesh, I become who I am—energy and spirit. I am not my mind. I am not my brain. I am stardust, comets, nebulae and galaxies. I am trees and wind and stone. I am space. I am emptiness and wholeness at the same time. That is when my body sings to me, a glorious ancient song redolent with mystery seeking to remain mystery. Connecting to it, living with it, becoming it even for a moment, I am healed and made more. Ceremony—whatever brings you closer to your essential self.

I DON'T WANT to touch you skin to skin. I want to touch you deeply, beneath the surface, where our real stories lie. Touch you where the fragments of our being are, where the sediment of things that shaped us forms the verdant delta of our human story. I want to bump against you and feel the rush of contact and ask important questions and offer compelling answers, so that together we might learn to live beneath the surface, where the current bears us forward deeper into the great ocean of shared experience. This is how I want to touch and be touched—through beingness—so that someday I might discover that even the skin remembers.

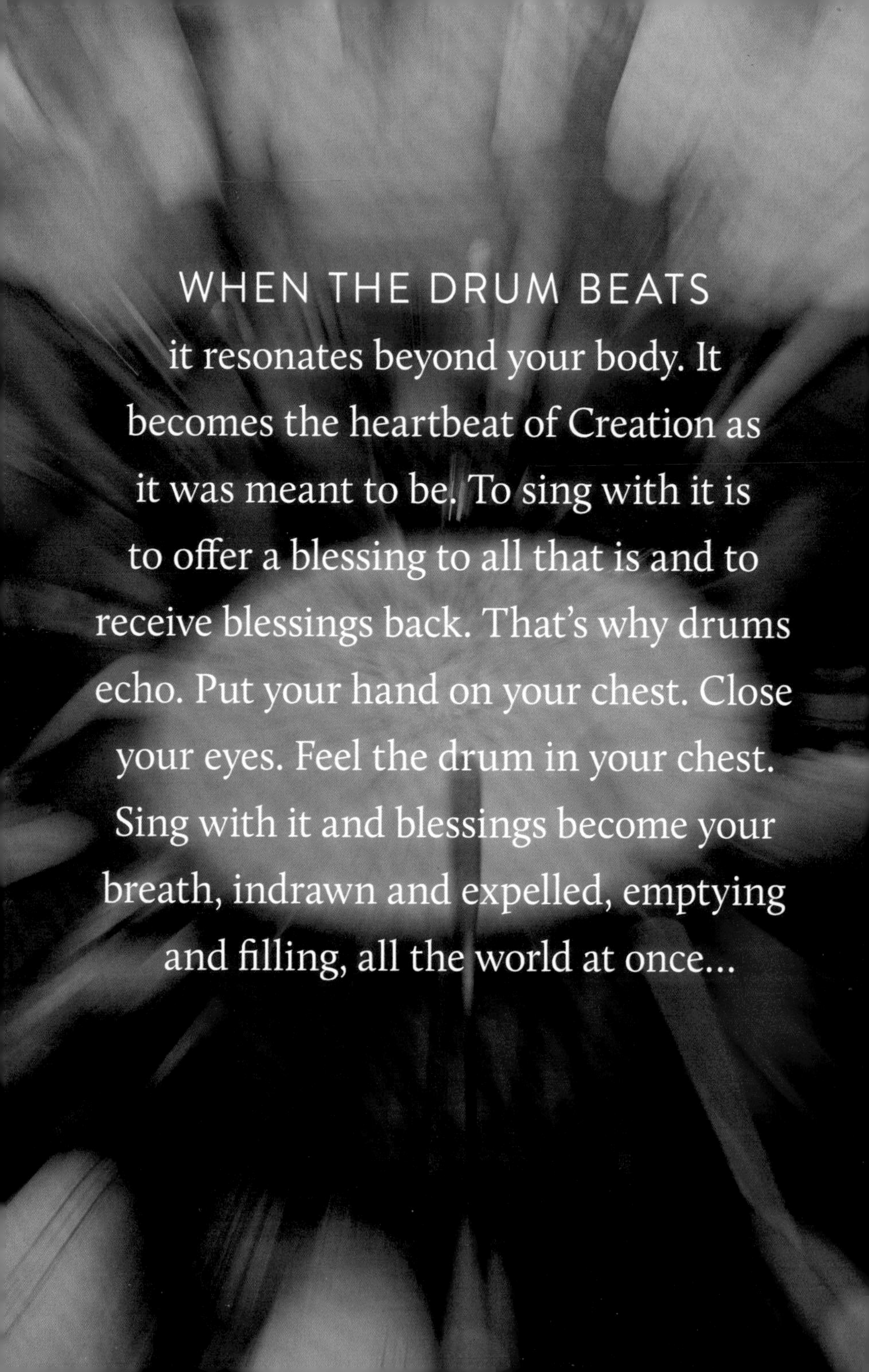

WHEN THE DRUM BEATS it resonates beyond your body. It becomes the heartbeat of Creation as it was meant to be. To sing with it is to offer a blessing to all that is and to receive blessings back. That's why drums echo. Put your hand on your chest. Close your eyes. Feel the drum in your chest. Sing with it and blessings become your breath, indrawn and expelled, emptying and filling, all the world at once...

III.

trust

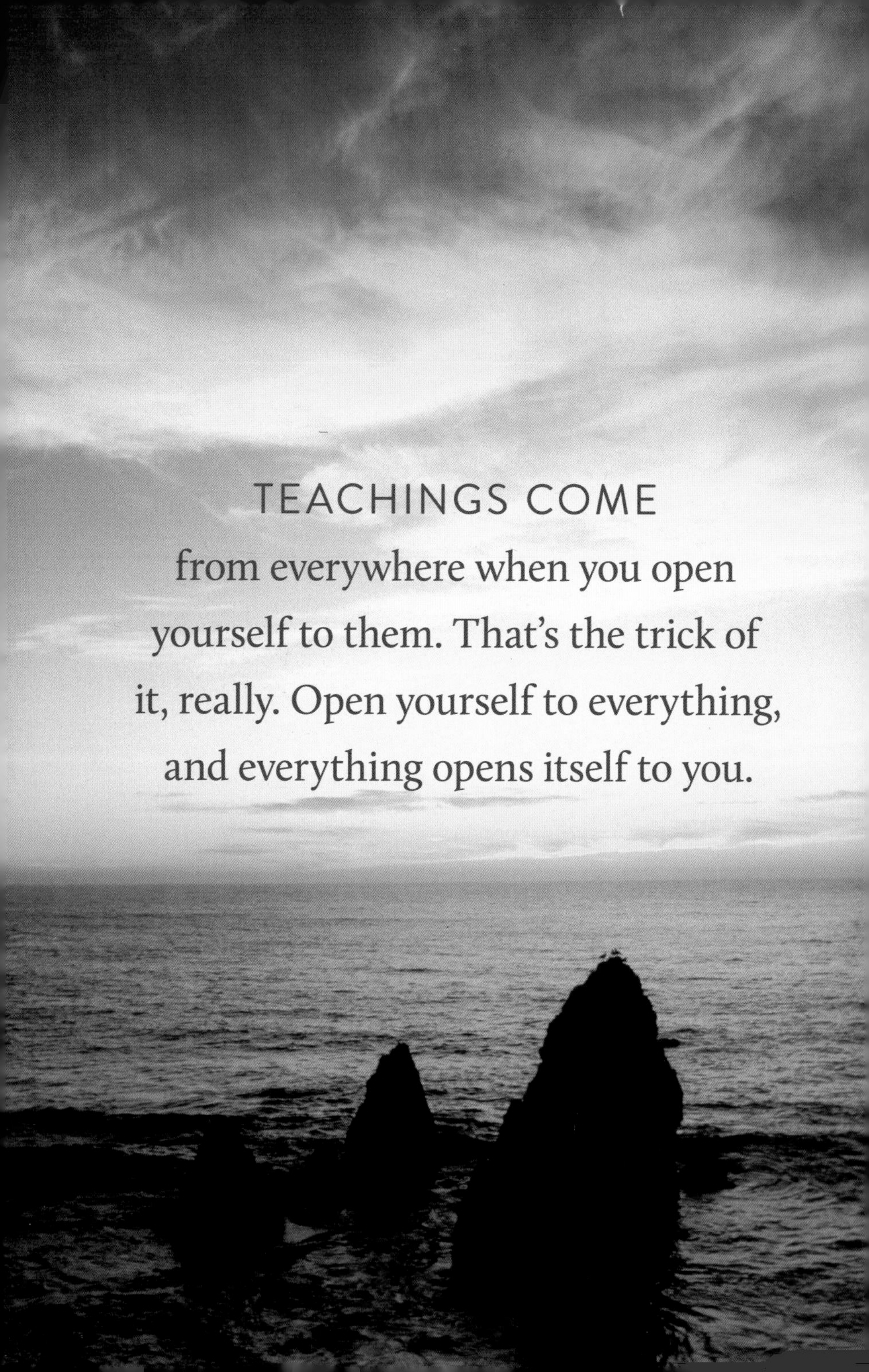

TEACHINGS COME from everywhere when you open yourself to them. That's the trick of it, really. Open yourself to everything, and everything opens itself to you.

ME: Sometimes, when things are hardest, it feels like Creator's not listening.

OLD WOMAN: Creator can do whatever Creator chooses. When we are in doubt or confusion or fear, She could send us thunderbolts or lightning or a huge pile of unexpected cash. But most of the time, she sends people. People are the miracles that emerge from the ripped and worn pattern of your life and help you stitch it back together. You learn to see the pattern better then.

THERE'S SOMETHING ELEMENTAL about sweet grass, sage, tobacco and cedar smouldering in an abalone bowl by the light of a single candle in the early morning dark. It reminds me of what is most important in my day: acknowledging and embracing the sacred. Without that, I can't walk out my door and discern the sacredness of other people. I can't be my own best self. Without that, I can't allow myself my limitations or allow others theirs. I can't be fair and loving and non-judgmental. Without that, I can't feel the depth and wonder of the mystery everywhere around me. I can't experience gratitude, worship or communion without that mystery. Those sacred moments of connection, when I choose to take them, are what set my feet on the path I hope to take right through my day. Some days, some moments, I stray from it—but I always know it's there.

ME: What does it mean to believe?

OLD WOMAN: It means to trust with your whole heart, to have faith. It means to have courage to act out of your belief.

ME: How do I do that?

OLD WOMAN: You have to be honest.

ME: What do you mean?

OLD WOMAN: You have to live your belief every day. To believe in something and not live it is dishonest.

***

I became a better human being after that.

A GIFT
IS NOT
a gift
UNTIL IT IS
shared

I AM IN the thrall of the power of words that spill out onto the page seemingly of their own accord. The lilt of the language reminds me that a gift is not a gift until it is shared, and I smile knowing that stories live in the soft curl of my knuckle. The keyboard comes alive with images, details, characters, and the presence of people that I have carved out of the ether and the sure, solid notion that Creator and my ancestors smile at each line of story splashed onto the pure-white dazzle of the page. Filling in the story, forming it, as I am filled and formed with each tapped letter crystallized into language.

FRIEND: What do I do when I don't like who I am?

ME: Hang out with people who do like who you are.

***

I think Old Woman would have been proud of my response.

THE SINGLE HARDEST lesson I've ever had to learn is that the greater, grander plan is not mine to create or know. If I am in ceremony and prayer for the right reasons, I leave all that up to Creator. When I surrender outcome, all things good and pure and peaceful come to me. My job is to choose what appears. Easy to say but hard to do, to get out of the way enough to allow the energy to flow.

SOMETIMES CREATOR BLINKS. Sometimes She is not looking at me. Those instances can feel really, really long some days, but what's going on is that Creator is showing Her trust in me. She's letting me know that I have the tools to cope with things, that I've learned enough in my walk with Her to walk gracefully through those moments when She blinks. And that's when I should blink, too. Close my eyes and breathe, feel the unceasing current underneath everything, surrender to it, then open my eyes again to possibility and walk on. That's how I learn to be graceful. Full of grace. In the blink of an eye.

ME: I can't seem to get anywhere in my life.

OLD WOMAN: Without Creator. Say what you said again, only add "without Creator" at the end.

ME: I can't seem to get anywhere in my life without Creator.

OLD WOMAN: Did you hear that? Anytime you're telling yourself there's something you can't do, can't solve, can't change, can't accept, say it out loud and add "without Creator." Add the same words to all the things you CAN do as well.

ME: I can get anywhere in my life with Creator.

OLD WOMAN: I think you're getting it, my boy.

WHEN MY ENERGY is low, meaning I don't feel at my best in terms of creativity, inspiration, attunement or rest, I let Creator have my flow and ask only to be a channel. My deepest audience connection has always happened when I do this. So, on my way to a podium nowadays, I say to myself, "Okay, Creator, you and me, one more time." When I surrender the delivery, along with the outcome, the anxiety and the expectation, everything becomes miraculous. It's a recipe for life, really.

WRITE SPONTANEOUSLY EVERY day for fifteen minutes.

First, get settled. Breathe. Big, deep, full breaths, taken slowly. Clear your mind of words. Be wordless. Then, open your eyes and write whatever comes out of you, and keep writing without taking your hands from the paper or the keyboard for fifteen minutes. Don't worry about punctuation or spelling. Just write. Every day. Fifteen minutes. Regardless. Watch what happens to your level of craft when you work on a project. Why? Because stories live in our bodies and we need to feel our fingers moving in the process of creation every day. Your hands are your interpretive tools. They bring your spirit out in words and language.

Be
WORDLESS

MY DEAL WITH CREATOR IS THIS: I'm dragging a sack of old worries, hurt, anger, doubt and fear up a long hill trying to get to the other side, to relief, to healing.

CREATOR SAYS, "If you need a hand, I'm here. You pull and I'll push."

I SAY, "Really?"

CREATOR SAYS, "I promise that I will always be there to help you. But there's a catch."

I SAY, "What's the catch?"

CREATOR SAYS, "You have to pull first."

MY LIFE HAS been changed by the use of a single word—"yes." Leaving school at sixteen, having only completed Grade 9, I was untrained and unskilled at anything. I struggled for years: homeless, in dire poverty, lost. Then one day a possibility was presented to me—to be a storyteller—and I said "yes." A journalism career, more than a dozen books and numerous honours later, it's all because of that yes. There are a thousand ways to say "no," "but," "I can't," "it's impossible," "it's too late," but there's only one way to say "yes." With your whole being. When you do that, when you choose that word, it becomes the most spiritual word in the universe...And your world can change.

TELL THE STORY for the story's sake. Leave your expectations, ego and doubt at the door and use the story's energy to do your work. If your worries matter that much, you can pick them back up when you're finished for the day.

HOME IS THE slumping drop of luggage on floors that bear the ghostly footprints of your motion. The light is a lambent thing that feels right on your shoulders, so that walking here after time away is a convergence of energies. Past, present and future allow you floating passage on the way to a collection of "now"s that beat in your chest, settle on you lightly, glitter in your eyes and lodge in your mind as reflection, introspection and awareness. The shadow of the one you were before you left occupies a space in the corner as you re-enter and engage fully in simple, effortless things you do every day with what you come to recognize as love.

KEEP WHAT'S TRUE in front of you, Old Man said. You won't get lost that way. I was asking about making my way through the bush. He was talking about making my way through life. Turns out, all these years later, it was the same conversation.

KEEP
WHAT'S
true
IN FRONT
OF YOU

MY MOTHER'S PHYSICAL death taught me that I didn't come here to master devastating situations, circumstances, changes, losses or even my own feelings. I came here to experience them. I came here for soul lessons and spirit teachings so that I could carry on in this wonderful spiritual journey we are all on, this teaching way, this blessing way. So that, in the end, I can, like my mother has done, return to the beauty that I was when I first arrived here.

ME: What is the point of prayer and meditation?

OLD WOMAN: To bring you closer to the Great Mystery.

ME: So I can understand it?

OLD WOMAN: No. So you can participate in it.

* * *

I grew up spiritually after that.

IT SEEMS TO me the act of being spiritual is simply the act of allowing myself to feel my spirit move. It's not a huge ideological or theological process. It's just opening myself to living and allowing myself to absorb and be absorbed at the same time. That means I can find Creator in a blues run, a dance sequence, a conversation, a baby's laugh, the sound of the wind in the trees and the immaculate silence of an empty room in the stillness of dawn. Like now, here, on the eighteenth floor of a hotel with the sky a seeming foot away from my face.

YOU CAN'T TEST your courage timidly. You have to run through the fire, arms waving, legs pumping and heart beating wildly with the effort of reclaiming something vital, lost, laid aside or just plain forgotten. When you do that, you discover that we shine most brightly in community, the whole bedraggled, worn, frayed and tattered lot of us, bound together forever by a shared courage, a family forged in the heat of earnest struggle.

LIFE IS A series of passageways we choose largely on faith and a healthy dose of hope. We hope that the hallway of our choosing leads us to magic: the inexplicable, the sudden, the uncontained. Not so that we can capture it, hold it, make it our own—but just so that we can feel it, even for an instant. Feel it and know the truth that the universe itself is magic. Hope that by our believing, our blind trust, our inherent innocence, someday, sometime, somewhere, that magic will become us, even fleetingly, and we touch the face of God.

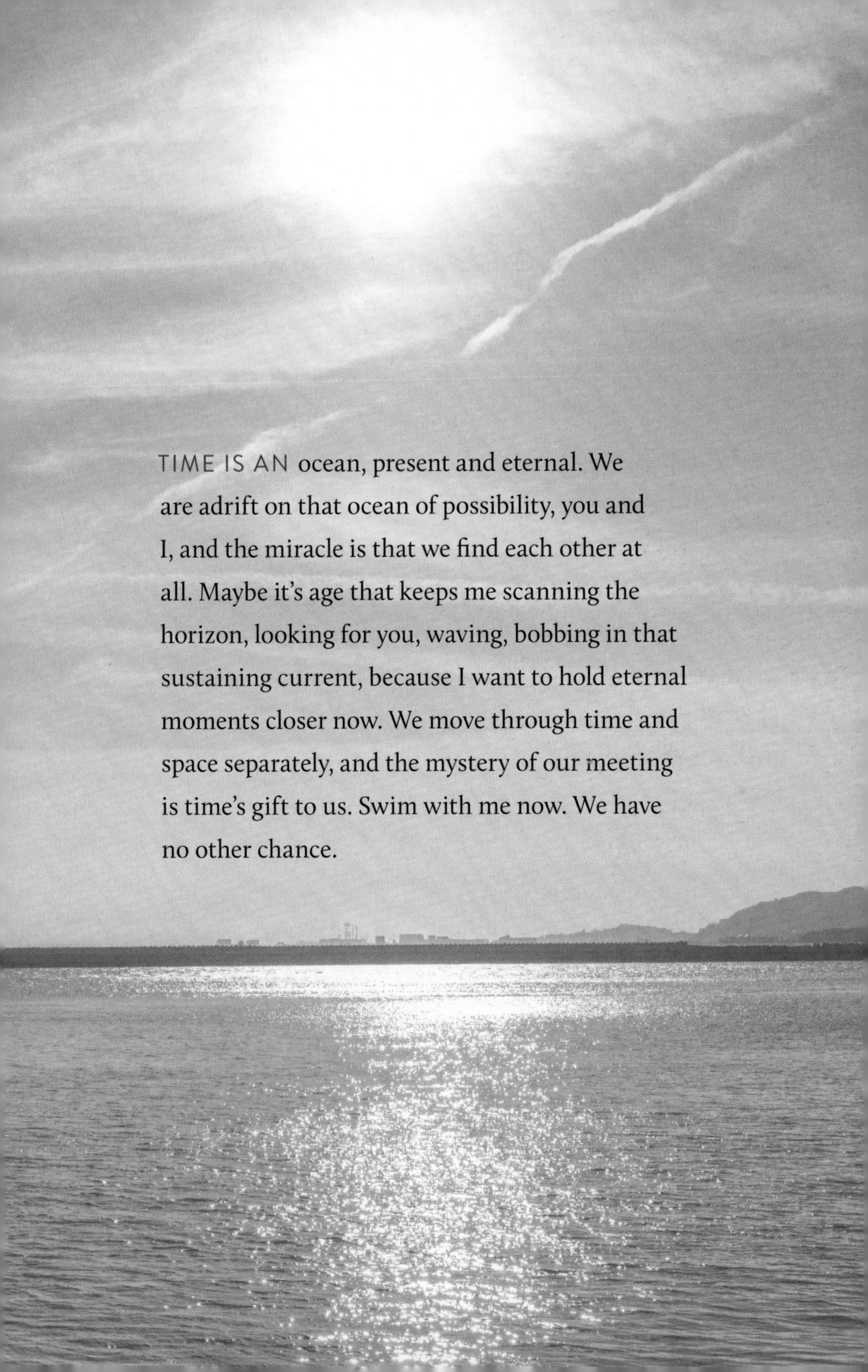

TIME IS AN ocean, present and eternal. We are adrift on that ocean of possibility, you and I, and the miracle is that we find each other at all. Maybe it's age that keeps me scanning the horizon, looking for you, waving, bobbing in that sustaining current, because I want to hold eternal moments closer now. We move through time and space separately, and the mystery of our meeting is time's gift to us. Swim with me now. We have no other chance.

EVERY RELATIONSHIP NEEDS a healthy dollop of spontaneity to keep it clicking. Nothing needs to be rehearsed or practised. There doesn't have to be a plan. One day, you just jump up and go, spinning into a rambunctious, off-the-cuff frolic. You don't check in, tweet, email or text while you're gone. There's no way to carry a cellphone on a skinny dip in the ocean, and you'd have to stop the wild energy to Instagram. Freedom is letting go of bounds and barriers, and hurling yourself into the adventure of living. That's how you build a book of moments, a love, a friendship, a family.

Freedom
IS LETTING GO of BOUNDS
AND BARRIERS,
& HURLING
YOURSELF
INTO THE adventure
of living

LIFE ISN'T SOMETHING you leave home to do. It's what you accomplish within the walls of your haven. That's what allows you to greet the world with an open heart and reach out and embrace living in all its richness, variety and staggering wonder.

ME: What's the hardest spiritual thing I'm ever going to have to do?

OLD WOMAN: To see every person as a gift.

ME: What kind of a gift?

OLD WOMAN: The best kind. Based on the way you receive them.

ME: I don't get it.

OLD WOMAN: I know. But you will. If you receive others as worthy, lovable, spiritual creations—perfect just the way they are—you get to see the highest possible version of who you are. You get to be that. Experience that. And you become a gift to the world.

ME: Sounds hard.

OLD WOMAN: The longer you think that, the harder it gets.

***

The funny thing is, she was right.

ME: Why does Creator test me sometimes?

OLD WOMAN: She doesn't. YOU test you.

ME: But I don't. Things just happen.

OLD WOMAN: And that's when you test yourself. Rather than trusting, you slip back into believing that Creator is not love but judgment. That's when you believe again that you can fail, that you need to prove your worthiness, when you reclaim fear as a driving energy.

ME: I don't feel like I do that.

OLD WOMAN: No one does. But Creator does not give you tests. What she gives you are opportunities to prove to yourself how much you want to change and grow. It's never Creator who needs the convincing.

* * *

This is what I carry into the future.

IV.

reverence

to live in
CEREMONY
is the
GREATEST
and
TRUEST GIFT
we can give to
OURSELVES

REMEMBER TO REMEMBER. This is what Old Man said to me one time. He was speaking of ceremony, of the act of bringing myself closer to Creator, returning myself to innocence, my original power. Remember to remember. He meant for me, throughout my day, to recall that I've taken the time to pray, to give thanks, to ask for a return to humility. Remember to remember. When I do that, everyone and everything I encounter becomes the beneficiary. It's a good teaching—as long as I remember.

FOR YOU TODAY, my friends, I raise sacred smoke. For you who are troubled, confused, doubtful, lonely, afraid, addicted, unwell, bothered or alone, I raise sacred smoke. For those of you in sorrow, grief or pain, I raise sacred smoke. For those who work for people, for change, for spiritual evolution, for the upward and outward growth of our common humanity and the well-being of our planet, I raise sacred smoke. For those of you in joy, in the glow of small or great triumphs, who live in love, faith, courage and respect, I raise sacred smoke. And, in the act of all of this, I raise it also for myself.

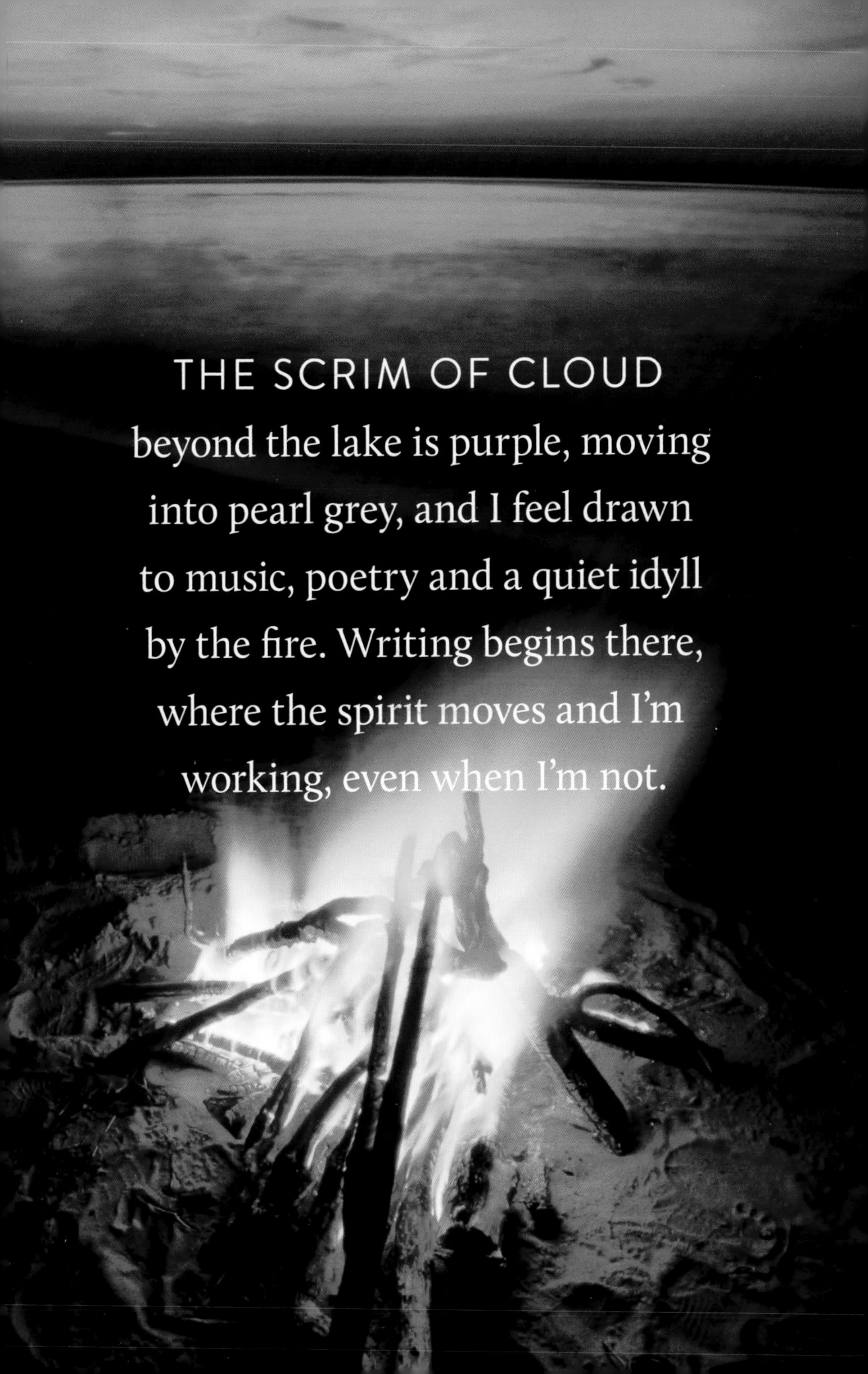

THE SCRIM OF CLOUD beyond the lake is purple, moving into pearl grey, and I feel drawn to music, poetry and a quiet idyll by the fire. Writing begins there, where the spirit moves and I'm working, even when I'm not.

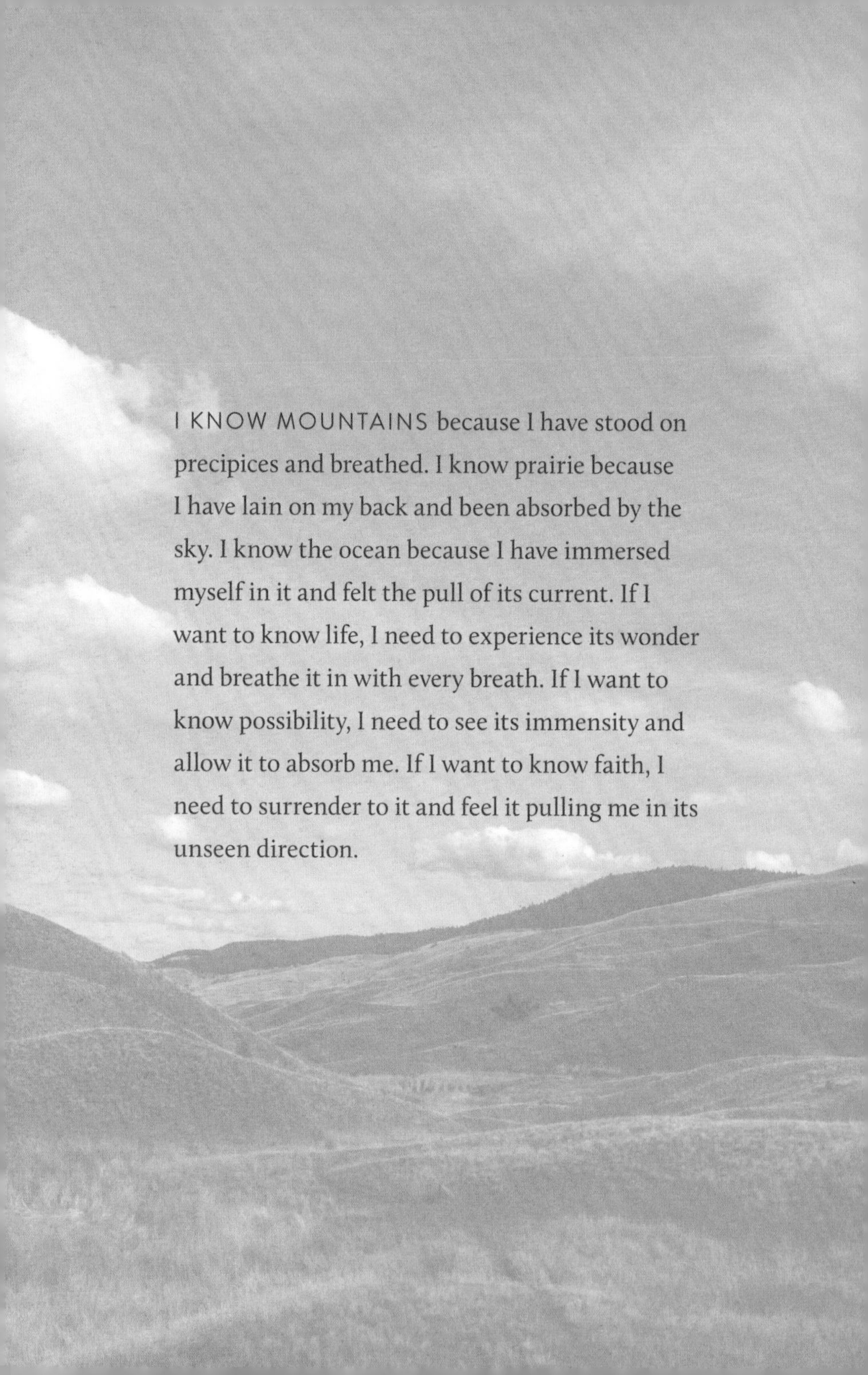

I KNOW MOUNTAINS because I have stood on precipices and breathed. I know prairie because I have lain on my back and been absorbed by the sky. I know the ocean because I have immersed myself in it and felt the pull of its current. If I want to know life, I need to experience its wonder and breathe it in with every breath. If I want to know possibility, I need to see its immensity and allow it to absorb me. If I want to know faith, I need to surrender to it and feel it pulling me in its unseen direction.

WHEN I WAS a kid, I dreamed of travelling the world. I called it "going to see." My adoptive parents laughed, assuming that I was misspelling a common word. I wasn't. The idea of the wide world filled me with wonder, and I wanted to see. I'm still like that. The world beckons me beyond wherever I am, and I want to see the intricate and the expansive, the gamut of emotions on people's faces, the secret life of animals, acts of love, the regal quiet of old people, children laughing, the acts of wonder that arise from Creator's hand in everything.

WAKE AND WATCH the universe shrug itself into wakefulness, as night surrenders slowly to day and shadow relinquishes itself to light. I watch this display and realize that the moon lives in the lining of my skin, the sun rises with my consciousness, and the earth thrums in the bottoms of my feet. Everywhere I go, I take that sense of wonder and mystery with me.

I'VE BEEN REFERRED to as odd before. Nowadays, I prefer to refer to myself as "awed." I want awe to be the greatest ongoing relationship in my life. I want to move through my days floored by the magnificence and generosity of my Creator. The breaking of a day, the silence between words, the light emanating from a real conversation, and kindness, truth, love and the apparently random hand of grace: I want to remain gobsmacked by all of it. Rendered speechless by wonder, I await the next unfolding. Peace, friends. Be awed today.

ME: I've been waiting for messages from Creator.

OLD WOMAN: They always come. But waiting is not seeing. Expecting is not feeling. Demanding is not hearing.

ME: I don't get it.

OLD WOMAN: I know. But those clouds are Creator's handwriting. That wolf track in the mud is Creator's touch. Those birds singing in the trees are Creator's voices. A drum beating or your own heartbeat is Creator's Morse code. Children and elders and life itself are Creator's exclamation marks.

***

I started to get the message after that.

YOU STOKE THE FIRES of creativity with humility, gratitude and awareness. You need to ask for the gift to be directed. Writing is a spiritual process. To be a creator you need to connect with Creator.

ME: Why do I use a drum?

OLD WOMAN: To touch the earth.

ME: Then why do I sing with it?

OLD WOMAN: To allow the earth to touch you.

ME: What am I singing for?

OLD WOMAN: So that someday you might sing the one note that joins your heartbeat and the earth's heartbeat to the heartbeat of everything.

ME: You're saying that drumming and singing, anything that leads me inward and then outward, are just like praying and meditating.

OLD WOMAN: You are getting wiser, my boy.

I CAME HERE to inhabit a body that would allow my soul to experience. So I am not my body. I came here to experience the grandest thought. So I am not my mind. I came here to experience the deepest feeling. So I am not my feelings. I am all of it: thought, feeling and experience. That translates to awe, joy and reverence. For all life, for all beings, for all Creation. Knowing this, understanding this, makes living the hardest thing of all—but the joy is in the challenge, the gradual day-by-day becoming.

THERE ARE TIMES IN YOUR life you are flung into an undiscovered country of being, a place beyond time and tide and detail, the full magical breath of you heaving with the indescribable joy of being, and you realize then that parts of you exist in exile and completeness is journeying to bring them home.

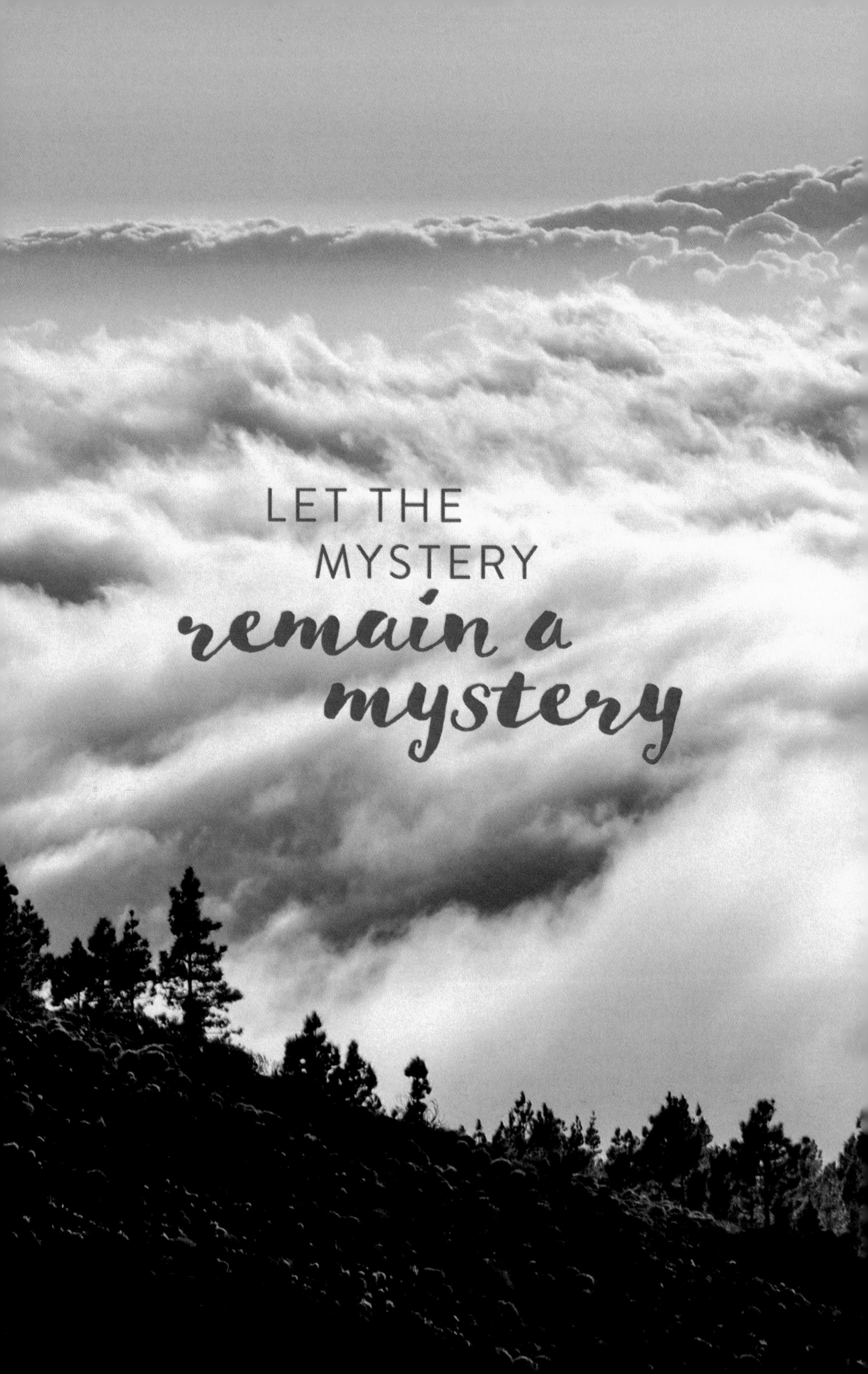
LET THE
MYSTERY
remain a
mystery

MY ELDERS SAY that the dream world is a reality, just as valid, just as vibrant, just as alive as the physical world. Dreams are not illusory things. They are meant to teach us, guide us. They ask us to use our intuition to interpret them. That's their biggest gift—returning us to our intuition, our highest level of thought. When we intuit, we think spiritually with a free, flowing energy. In the physical world, that's where compassion is born—the place where there are no differences. Dream big, bright and shining. Enjoy the images. Intuition will teach you meaning.

ON MY MORNING walk, the mountain said, "Let the mystery remain a mystery. Grace comes with finding your path to it every day. Power comes from embracing that." It was a good morning walk...

WRITING IN THE last frail dark of winter's morning and the words seem to tumble from that waning dark and onto the bright, white light of the page. This is where poetry is born. The song that is language emerging beat by beat, declaring itself. And you, swaddled in wonder, breathing in the depths of the Great Mystery and exhaling story one hen peck at a time, scratching the surface of what lies beneath to frame the world again into something you can recognize.

THERE ARE PERIODS when you exist beyond the context of time and fact and reality. Moments when memory carries you buoyant beyond all things, and life exists as fragments and shards of being, when you see yourself as you were and will be again—sacred, whole and shining.

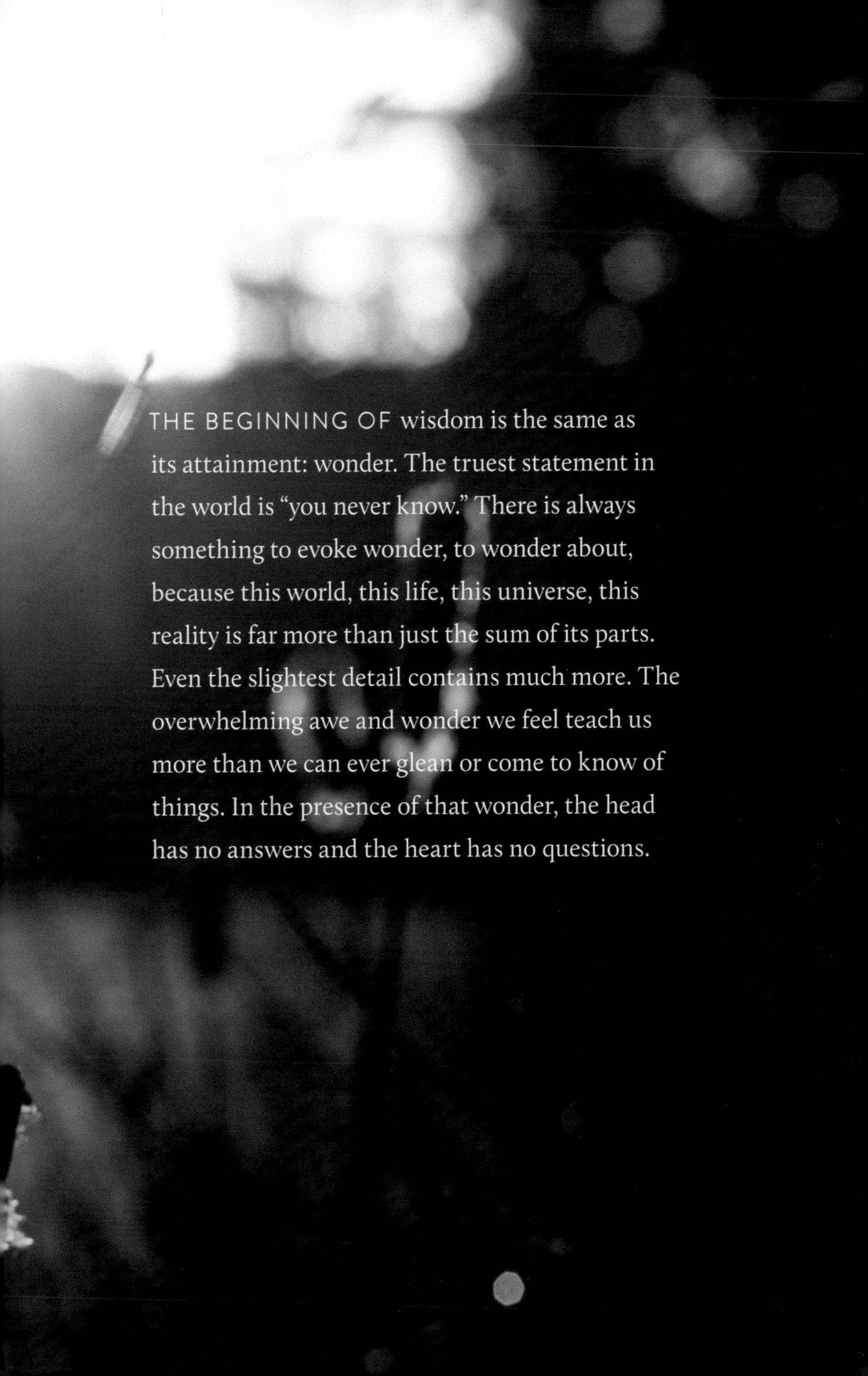

THE BEGINNING OF wisdom is the same as its attainment: wonder. The truest statement in the world is "you never know." There is always something to evoke wonder, to wonder about, because this world, this life, this universe, this reality is far more than just the sum of its parts. Even the slightest detail contains much more. The overwhelming awe and wonder we feel teach us more than we can ever glean or come to know of things. In the presence of that wonder, the head has no answers and the heart has no questions.

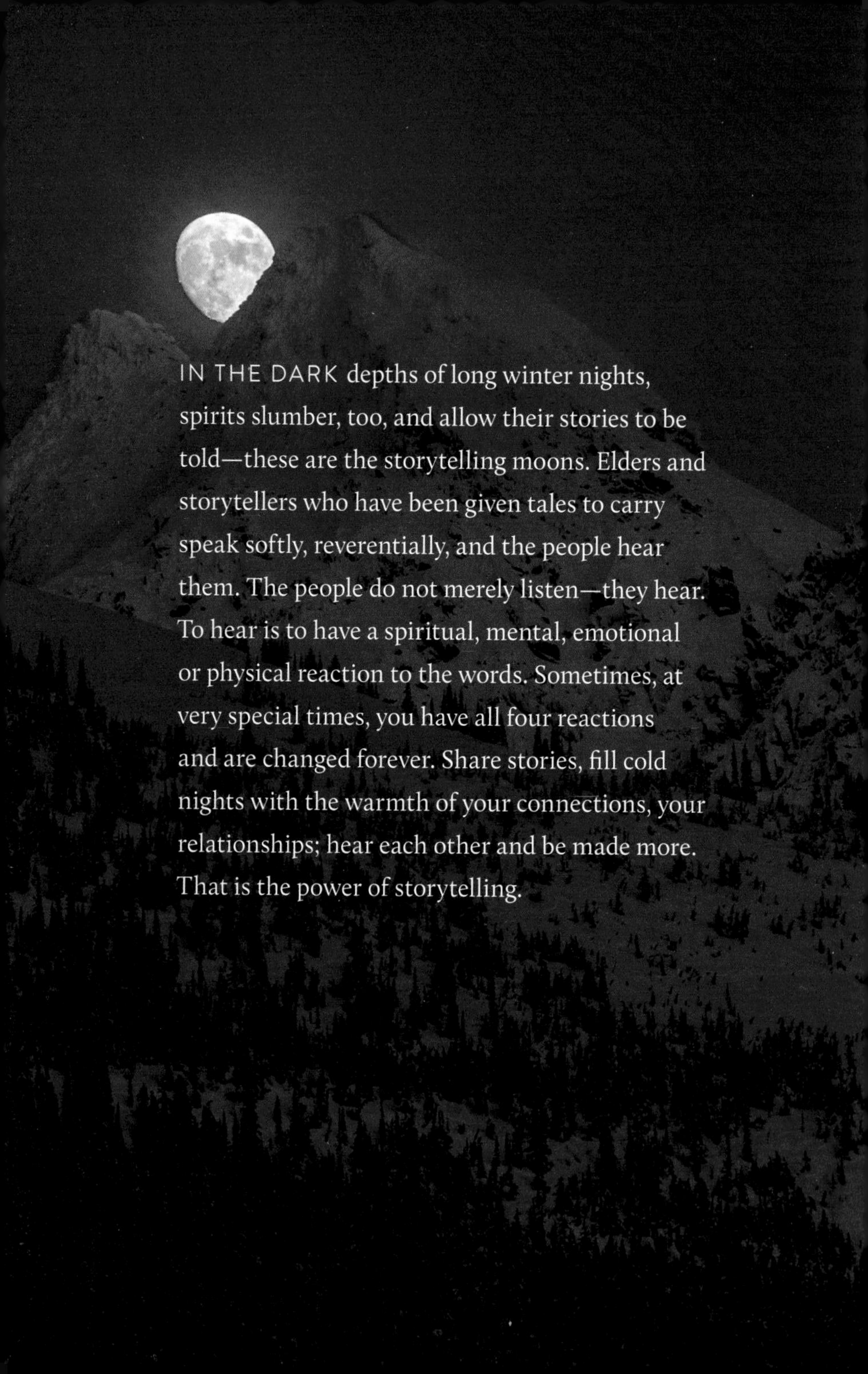

IN THE DARK depths of long winter nights, spirits slumber, too, and allow their stories to be told—these are the storytelling moons. Elders and storytellers who have been given tales to carry speak softly, reverentially, and the people hear them. The people do not merely listen—they hear. To hear is to have a spiritual, mental, emotional or physical reaction to the words. Sometimes, at very special times, you have all four reactions and are changed forever. Share stories, fill cold nights with the warmth of your connections, your relationships; hear each other and be made more. That is the power of storytelling.

REMEMBER. REMEMBER THAT Creator is the wind on my face, the rain in my hair, the sun that warms me. Creator is the trees, rocks, grasses, the majesty of the sky and the intense mystery of the universe. Creator is the infant who giggles at me in the grocery line, the beggar who reminds me how rich I really am, the idea that fires my most brilliant moment, the feeling that fuels my most loving act and the part of me that yearns for that feeling again and again. Whatever ceremony, ritual, meditation, song, thought or action it takes to reconnect to that feeling is what I need to do today...Remember.

TO BE STRUCK by the magnificence of nature is to be returned again, in all-too-brief moments, to the innocence in which we were born. Awe. Wonder. Humility. We draw them into us and are altered forever by the unquestionable presence of Creator. All things ringing true together. If we carry that deep sense of communion back into our workaday lives, everyone we meet benefits. That is what we are here for: to remind each other of where the truth lies and the power of simple ceremony.

IN THE DEEP snow moons of winter, there are stories hovering around us. They are whispered by the voices of our ancestors, told in ancient tongues, told in the hope that we will hear them. Listen. In the drape of moonbeams across a canvas of snow, the lilt of birdsong, the crackle of a fire, the smell of smudge and the echo of the heartbeats of those around us, our ancestors speak to us, call to us, summon us to the great abiding truth of stories: that simple stories, well told, are the heartbeat of the people. Past. Present. Future.

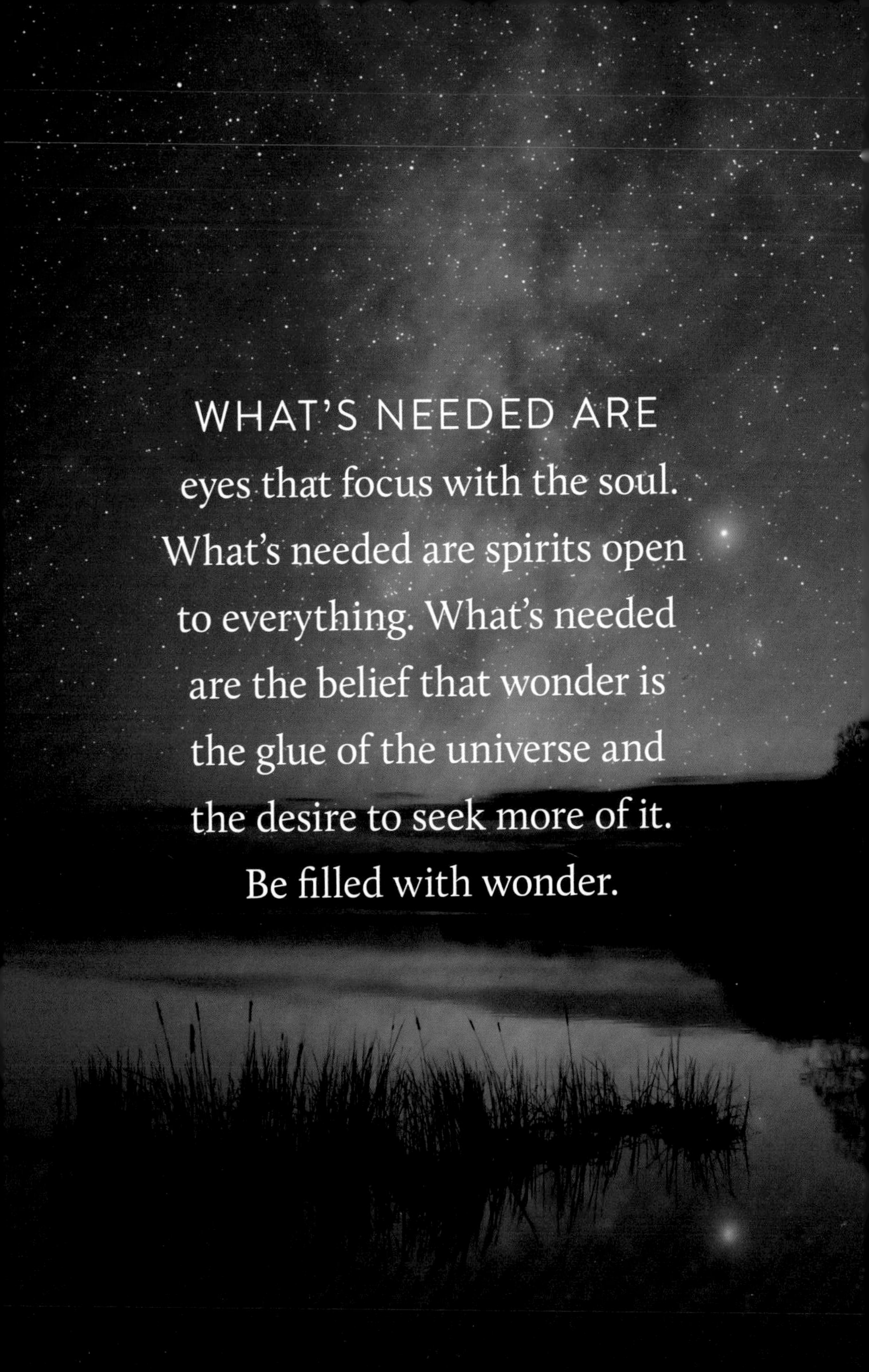

WHAT'S NEEDED ARE eyes that focus with the soul. What's needed are spirits open to everything. What's needed are the belief that wonder is the glue of the universe and the desire to seek more of it. Be filled with wonder.

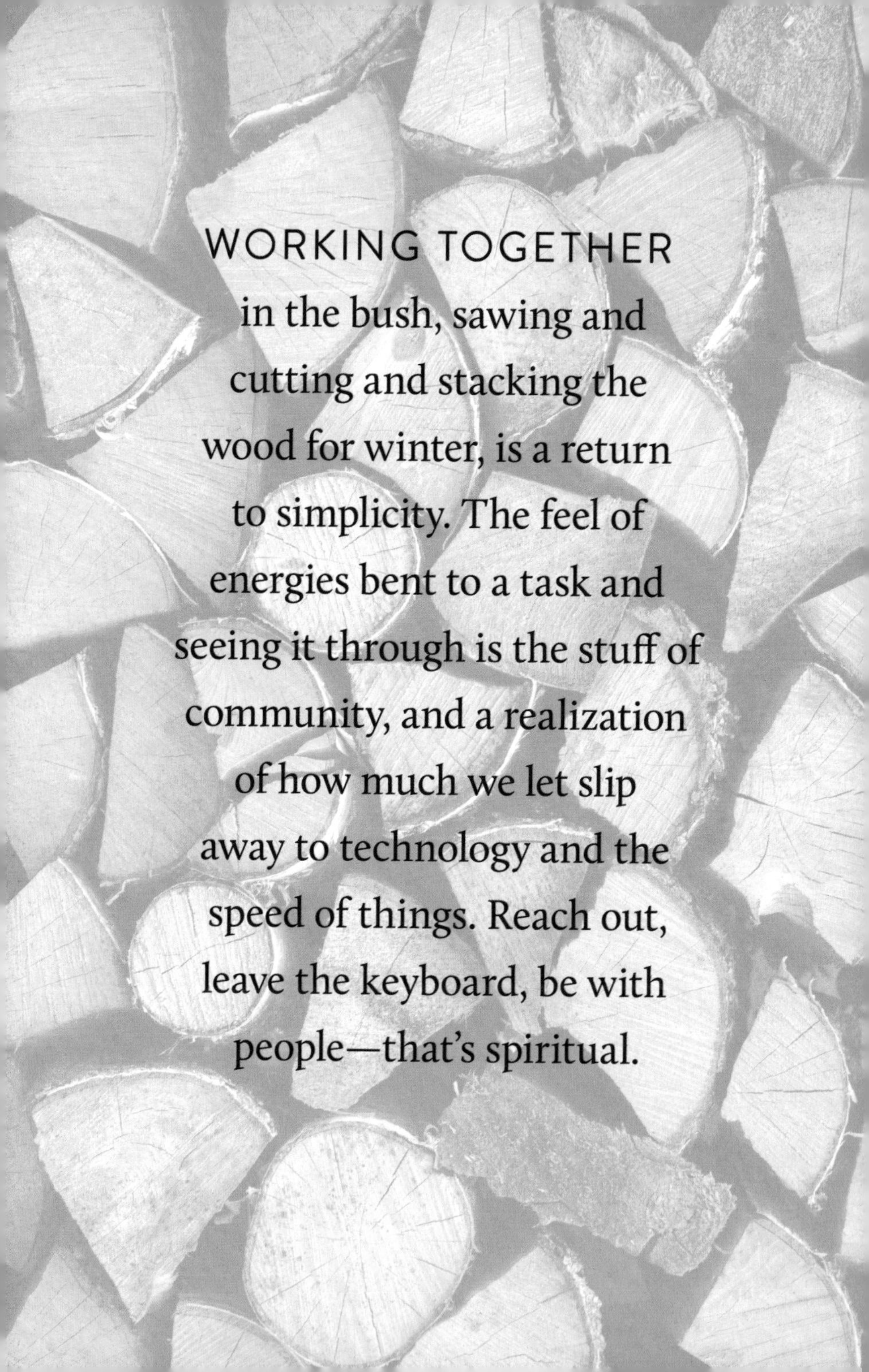

WORKING TOGETHER in the bush, sawing and cutting and stacking the wood for winter, is a return to simplicity. The feel of energies bent to a task and seeing it through is the stuff of community, and a realization of how much we let slip away to technology and the speed of things. Reach out, leave the keyboard, be with people—that's spiritual.

V.

persistence

OLD MAN: You know what your problem is, Wagamese?

ME: No.

OLD MAN: That's what your problem is.

***

I became a better person after that.

I NO LONGER want to be resilient. I don't want to simply bounce back from things that hurt me or cause me pain. Bouncing back means returning to where I stood before. Instead, I want to go beyond the hurts and the darkness. The first step toward genuine healing from my mental illness was when I came to trust and believe that there was a beyond. Now I reach for beyond every day, in every encounter, in every circumstance. I seek to go where I have never travelled. I wake with the vision of a purposeful day, filled with adventures and teachings. Then I take the first step and try to make it Beyond.

TAKE THE
first step
& TRY TO
make it
Beyond

ME: What is the point of all this ceremony, this prayer, this damn hard work?

OLD WOMAN: To awaken from the dream.

ME: What dream is that?

OLD WOMAN: The illusion that what we see is all there is. That this physical world is the real one.

ME: Are there higher dreams, then?

OLD WOMAN: Yes. Dreams of unity over aloneness, blessings over fear, freedom over blame, unlimited spiritual possibility over limited material gain.

ME: You're telling me all that is possible?

OLD WOMAN: I'm telling you to choose to awaken. All is possible once you do that.

WHEN THERE'S A crack in my mirror, I can't see myself as I am—all I see is the crack. The crack tells me that there is something wrong with me, that I'm not enough and that this is how others see me, too. It's not a question of finding a better mirror. It's about seeing beyond the crack. I am not, nor ever will be, perfect. But I don't need to live for approval. I need to live for acceptance and joy in the unique, worthy, lovable, beautiful, sacred being that I am and to celebrate the same thing in others. That's seeing beyond the crack. I'm learning to love my imperfections; in the end, they make me who I am, in all my flawed glory.

IT'S ALL ABOUT OPENING, really. When I open myself to the world and its possibilities—even its hurts—I become whole. But when I choose to close, my life becomes fraught with struggle. Everything I do becomes about shielding myself rather then inviting good energy to fill me. Everything is energy, so I try to let the negative pass through me, rather than holding on to it.

ME: You always repeat things three times.

OLD WOMAN: Just the important things.

ME: Why? I hear you the first time.

OLD WOMAN: No. You listen the first time. You hear the second time. And you feel the third time.

ME: I don't get it.

OLD WOMAN: When you listen, you become aware. That's for your head. When you hear, you awaken. That's for your heart. When you feel, it becomes a part of you. That's for your spirit. Three times. It's so you learn to listen with your whole being. That's how you learn.

ME: What's the greatest teaching in life?

OLD WOMAN: You have to make your own moccasins.

ME: You're kidding, right?

OLD WOMAN: No. You make them from the hide of your experience, all the places you have walked. You sew them with the thread of the teachings, the lessons embedded in all the hard miles. You stitch them carefully with the needle of your intention—to walk a spiritual path—and when you're finished, you realize that Creator lives in the stitches. That's what helps you walk more gracefully.

***

I got busy learning how to sew.

I AM NOT the endless chatter in my head. I am the me who recognizes that chatter is happening. I am not the me who is impatient in the grocery line or at the stoplight. I am the me who recognizes and acknowledges that impatience. If I take a breath and change the chatter to "This is me waiting calmly," that is what the experience becomes. Practising this simple awareness allows me to be present in all moments, to fully inhabit my life.

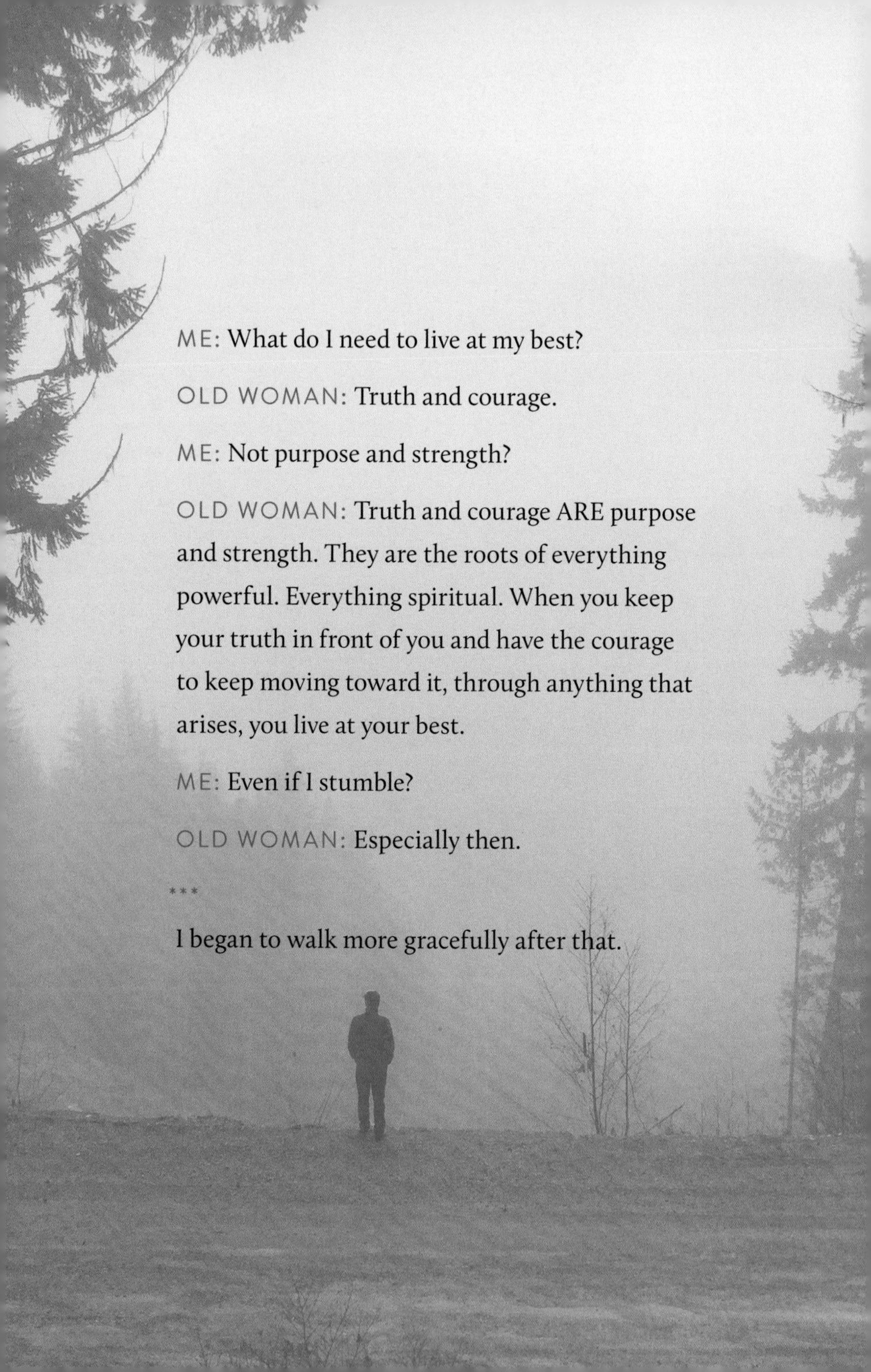

ME: What do I need to live at my best?

OLD WOMAN: Truth and courage.

ME: Not purpose and strength?

OLD WOMAN: Truth and courage ARE purpose and strength. They are the roots of everything powerful. Everything spiritual. When you keep your truth in front of you and have the courage to keep moving toward it, through anything that arises, you live at your best.

ME: Even if I stumble?

OLD WOMAN: Especially then.

***

I began to walk more gracefully after that.

I LIVE FOR miracles in my life these days. Not the earth-changing, light-bringing, soul-powering kind. But the ones that carve out a small space of peace where before there was only the jumble of resentment, fear and doubt. The ones that happen from choosing to live the right way. Like coming to understand that forgiveness isn't about gaining a release from others—it's about gaining release from me. If I release my hold on what binds me, I can walk free and unencumbered. But I have to embrace the resentment, fear and doubt to gain that. I have to own them, hold them again, so that I can learn to let them go. In that letting go is the miracle.

OLD WOMAN: You can't fix what's in your head using what's in your head.

ME: What do I do, then?

OLD WOMAN: Unlearn.

ME: How do I do that?

OLD WOMAN: Choose differently.

YOU STAND ON the edge of a canyon and you shout something. The world and the universe echo your own voice back, whether you shout "Yahoo!" or "Yee-haw!" That's how echoes work. What you throw out echoes your own energy back. "I love you." "Thank you, Creator!" "I am happy!" Such a small thing to consider but such a large thing to do. Which words am I throwing out to the universe today, and what will come back to me as a result?

SHOUT
something.

ME: Tell me about love.

OLD WOMAN: It is our only real choice. The only thing that we can truly give.

ME: How do we do that?

OLD WOMAN: Choose it above all else. Love is you leading me back to the highest possible version of myself. It's me leading you back to who you were created to be. It is the most important choice we can make for each other.

ME: Those closest to us, you mean.

OLD WOMAN: No. Everyone. Everything. Widening our circle at every opportunity.

ME: Sounds hard.

OLD WOMAN: So is being born. But we all do it.

SOMEONE ONCE ASKED me what I mean when I say, "Stay Brown." Well, my people say that life is a circle. They say that we are a part of all of life. They also say that, as a part of all of life, we are creating our lives every instant we are here. My spiritual father taught me this way: What I think I create. What I create I become. What I become I express. What I express I experience. What I experience I am. And so on and so on and so on. That's the circle moving. My responsibility to myself and to life is to act as though I believe this until I do believe it. So, stay Brown. Be the circle moving...

ME: How do I find Creator?

OLD WOMAN: You become what you seek.

ME: I don't understand.

OLD WOMAN: You decide what Creator is. If you decide She is peace, love, humility and non-judgment, you decide to work toward embodying those qualities in your walkabout world. The closer you get to that, the closer you are to finding Creator. That's what our ceremonies are for. To teach you that Creator is in you, that She always was and always will be.

SOMETHING THAT MOST do not understand about my people: when we stand up in acts of resistance to things that threaten our spiritual, physical, emotional and intellectual well-being, it's not because we hate what's in front of us—it's because we love what's behind us. We love our homes, our families, our communities, our nations, our ceremonies, our teachings, our cultural ways, our histories and the land that those things spring from. In that, we are like anyone anywhere throughout the course of human history who has ever stood up to injustice. Stay Brown!

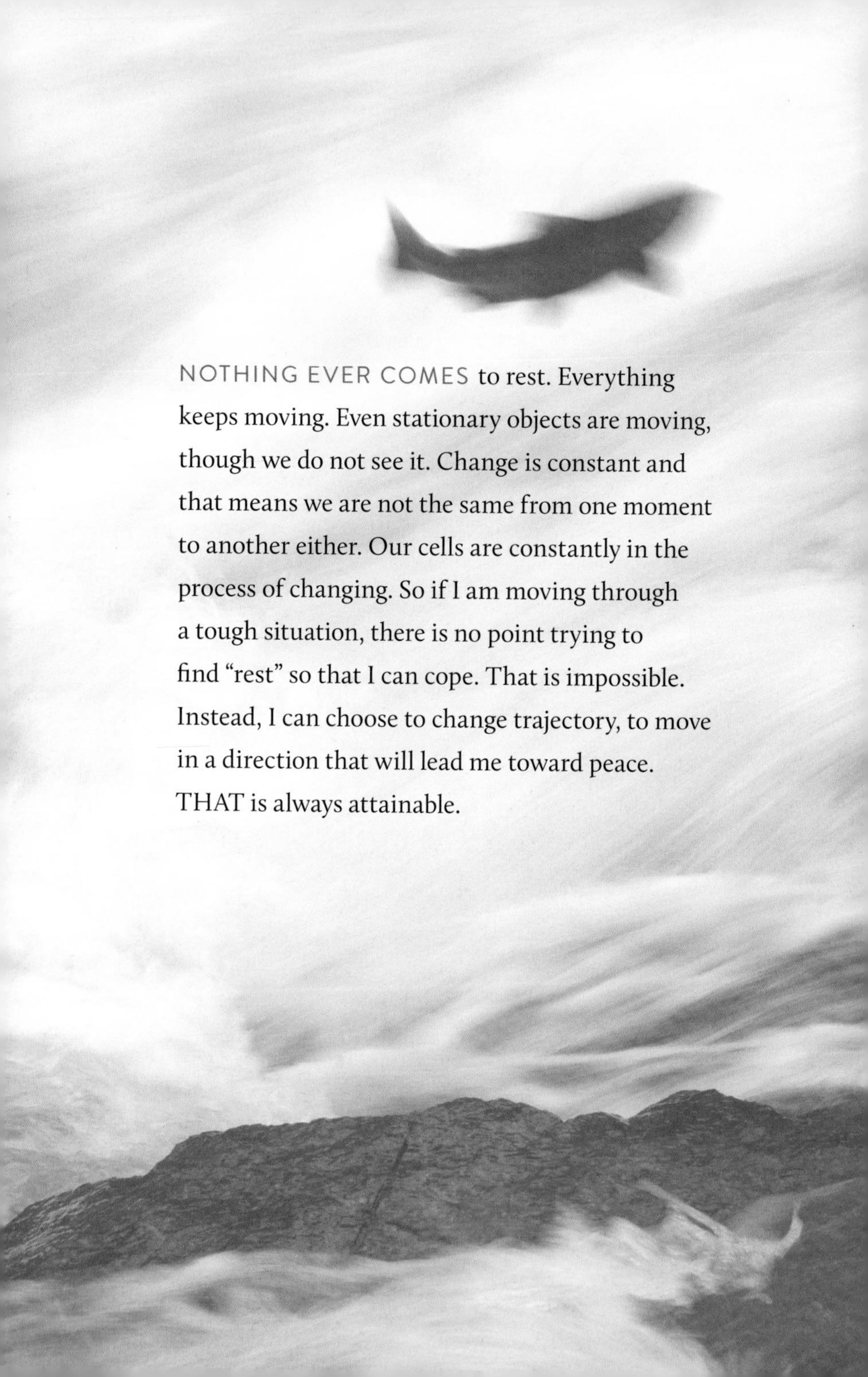

NOTHING EVER COMES to rest. Everything keeps moving. Even stationary objects are moving, though we do not see it. Change is constant and that means we are not the same from one moment to another either. Our cells are constantly in the process of changing. So if I am moving through a tough situation, there is no point trying to find "rest" so that I can cope. That is impossible. Instead, I can choose to change trajectory, to move in a direction that will lead me toward peace. THAT is always attainable.

THE TRUTH IS that I have physical, mental, emotional, spiritual and moral limitations. But physically, I want to be healthy enough to do good work. Mentally, I want to be clear so that I can let go of thoughts that do not serve me. Emotionally, I want to be aware of my feelings, so that I can surrender those that do not empower me. Spiritually, I want to walk in awe, wonder, respect and humility through this universe. Morally, I want to be a male human being I can be proud of. I don't need to know what perfect looks like—only better. I can move gracefully toward better every day.

SOMETIMES YOU WRITE just to feel your fingers moving. Sometimes all you need is the physical testament of the process that lives within you like a latent gene, expressed by the grip and release of fingers against the pale, open range of the page. There is the knowledge in you then of the infinite, wondrous worlds and people available to you.

ME: What is the secret to life?

OLD WOMAN: Learning to love it.

ME: Even the hard parts? Even the pain?

OLD WOMAN: Especially those. When you reach out to the love of living, instead of the fear of dying, you create more life.

ME: That sounds like hard work.

OLD WOMAN: Choose moments, then—and let the days take care of themselves.

YEARS AGO, I would copy passages by great writers in longhand. I copied pages and pages of writing I admired, because I wanted to experience what it must have felt like to create something excellent. I have little schooling, but that helped make me a good, strong writer in the end. These days, I do the same with spirituality. I copy what the great ones do or have done. I practise. Every day. I work hard at being selfless, honest, kind, generous, patient, open and compassionate. It's what makes me a good, strong human being.

ME: What does it mean to recover?

OLD WOMAN: It is to be reborn. We arrive here covered in spiritual qualities like innocence, humility, trust, acceptance and love. But things happen and those qualities get removed from us. Those qualities get churched off, spanked off, schooled off and beaten off. Sometimes we rinse them off ourselves with drugs and booze and poor choices. But when we start to walk with Creator again, we're graced with the opportunity to re-cover ourselves in those qualities.

ME: Does it hurt?

OLD WOMAN: Sometimes. But that's what makes the journey so magical.

ME: The hurt?

OLD WOMAN: No. The days you wake up without it.

ME: How will I know what's true for me?

OLD WOMAN: Choose. Then believe. Then act. Only you know the workings of your heart. Choose what your heart draws you to, not what your mind decides. Choose that every day until you come to believe in it. Then act out of that belief. That's how you will come to know your truth.

KNOWLEDGE IS NOT wisdom. But wisdom is knowledge in action. I have lived most of my years immersed in the culture of books. I command a lot of facts. I comprehend a lot of concepts. That does not make me wise or even intelligent. It just indicates what I have memorized. But when I activate those facts and concepts to find the greatest, grandest version of myself, and then use them to work toward that vision, I begin the process of wisdom. The most essential question to ask myself is not "What do I think about this?" but rather "How do I feel about this?" In such simplicity is greatness made possible for an individual, a society and a human family.

ME: Can I fail at spirituality?

OLD MAN: No. You were always spiritual.

ME: How do I get better at it?

OLD MAN: By remembering that deciding is not doing and wanting is not choosing.

ME: I don't get it.

OLD MAN: Move in the direction that brings you closer to Creator in all things. The trail will be revealed and the helpers will come to you.

ME: That's it?

OLD MAN: It is more than enough for one lifetime.

MY GAUGE EACH day, in all things, is simply this: Is what I'm choosing (to think, do or say) moving me closer to my Creator or farther away? For this question, I am immensely thankful. It saves me an awful lot of backtracking, worry lines, frustration, angst and apologizing. Today and every day, I give thanks for my ability to exercise the power of choice—even when I've chosen wrong.

HOW TO MAKE a dream come true: Don't focus on the dream, or it will always remain a dream. Instead, focus on the first action you can take to bring that dream a little closer. Then take it. Now focus on the next action, and take that. Each step brings the dream closer to becoming reality. Why? Our elders teach that the dream world and the real world operate on the same energy. You link them through the power of choice. Choose action and the dream moves ever closer to the real.

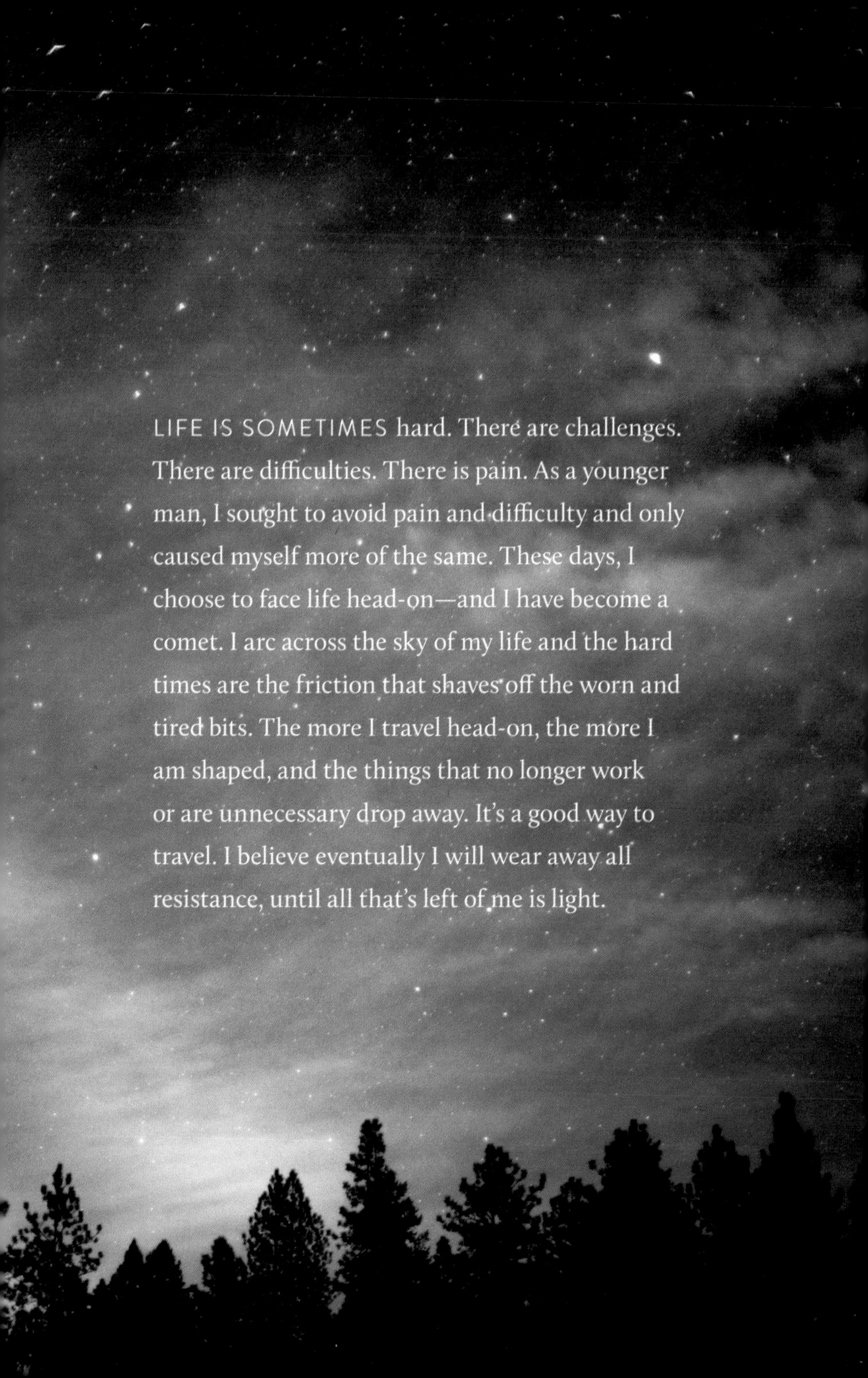

LIFE IS SOMETIMES hard. There are challenges. There are difficulties. There is pain. As a younger man, I sought to avoid pain and difficulty and only caused myself more of the same. These days, I choose to face life head-on—and I have become a comet. I arc across the sky of my life and the hard times are the friction that shaves off the worn and tired bits. The more I travel head-on, the more I am shaped, and the things that no longer work or are unnecessary drop away. It's a good way to travel. I believe eventually I will wear away all resistance, until all that's left of me is light.

ME: When are things going to get easier?

OLD WOMAN: They already are.

ME: Doesn't feel like it. I keep waiting for Creator to step in.

OLD WOMAN: She already has. She always will. Keep faith burning in your heart.

ME: I have. I've been waiting for things to change.

OLD WOMAN: Faith isn't about waiting for things to change. Faith is the constant effort to keep pushing through.

ME: What's on the other side?

OLD WOMAN: You.

VI.

gratitude

I ASK FOR
nothing
I ONLY OFFER
thanks

I RAISE THE pipe of my being to the rising sun in openness and humility. With my eyes closed, I give thanks to the Life Giver and ask for the strength to be humble through the course of this day. I smudge myself with sacred medicines and give thanks for the blessings that are already present in my life. I ask for nothing. I only offer thanks. Then, in gratitude and humility, I enter the journey of each day. This is wakefulness, this is becoming, this is ceremony—and I am made more.

WATCHING MORNING BREAK, I realize again that darkness doesn't kill the light—it defines it. I believe that now. For years, I didn't. I believed that I was my failures, mistakes, misjudgments, shortcomings and wrongs. But I'm not those things. I am the light that shines from my faith, my courage, my willingness to be vulnerable and to be responsible and accountable. Moments of darkness only highlight that truth these days. I'm moving beyond shame. I'm basking in the light of my own recovery and the brilliance that comes from allowing myself to be seen as I am, warts and all. I'm not just those warts, either—I'm the frog who wears them, gradually becoming a prince.

ME: What if we're wrong?

OLD WOMAN: Wrong about what?

ME: All this ceremony, prayer, meditation. What if, at the end of it, all there is is nothing?

OLD WOMAN: Then we still come out better people.

ME: How?

OLD WOMAN: Can you think of a better way to live than in gratitude? Can you think of a better way to be than to be kind, loving, compassionate, respectful, courageous, truthful and forgiving? Even if we're wrong, can you think of a better way to breathe than through all that?

***

I couldn't. I can't. I continue...

I'M LEARNING THAT happiness is an emotion that's a result of circumstances. Joy, though, is a spiritual engagement with the world based on gratitude. It's not the big things that make me grateful and bring me joy. It's more the glory of the small: a touch, a smile, a kind word spoken or received, that first morning hug, the sound of friends talking in our home, the quiet that surrounds prayer, the smell of sacred medicines burning, sunlight on my face, the sound of birds and walking mindfully, each footfall planted humbly on the earth.

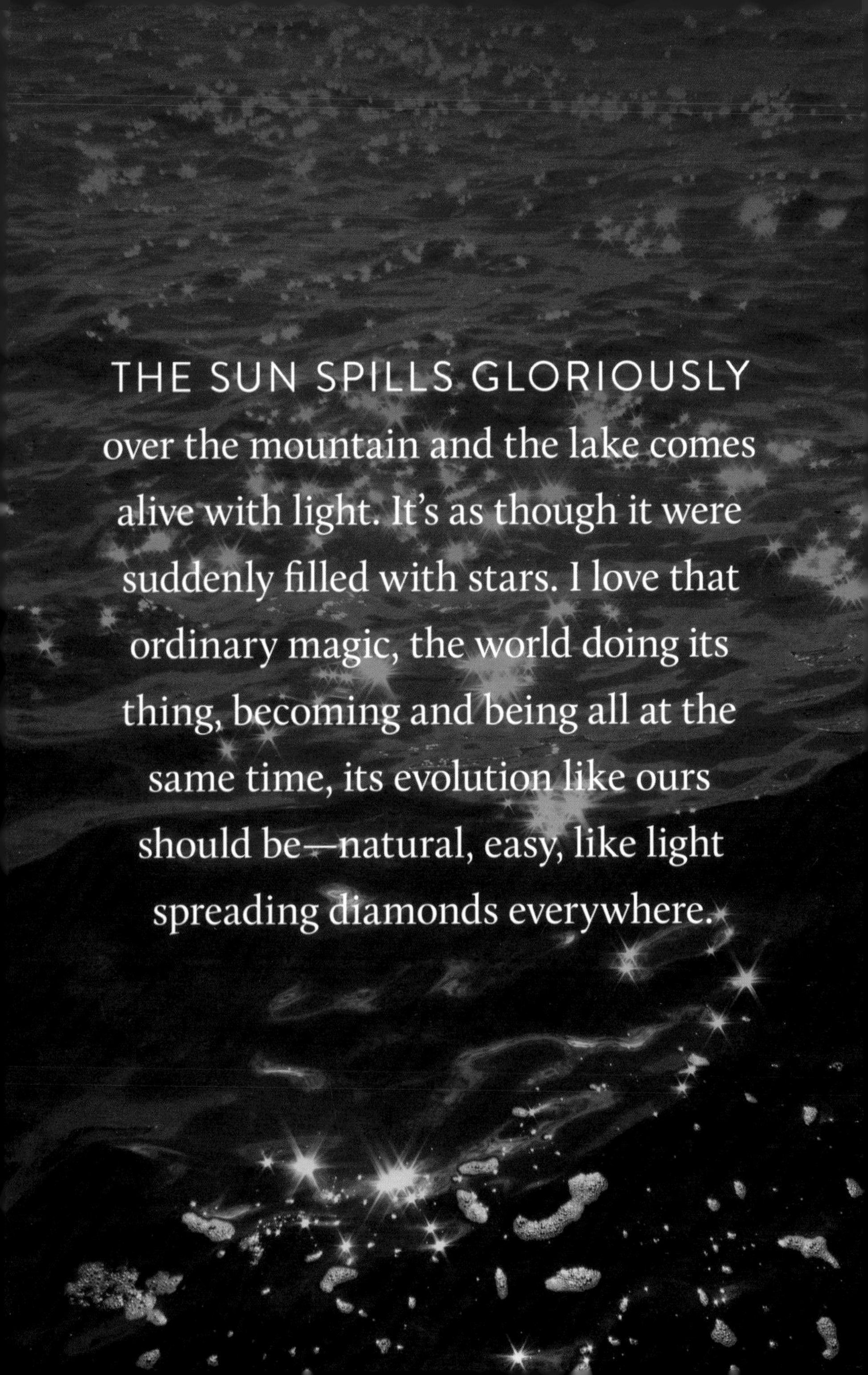

THE SUN SPILLS GLORIOUSLY over the mountain and the lake comes alive with light. It's as though it were suddenly filled with stars. I love that ordinary magic, the world doing its thing, becoming and being all at the same time, its evolution like ours should be—natural, easy, like light spreading diamonds everywhere.

MY FAVOURITE SIGHTS when addressing our people as a speaker are (1) elders smiling and nodding at words that come from our teachings, knowing that the generation behind them has been listening and will be okay, and (2) the younger generation behind me smiling, nodding, absorbing words that come from our teachings, listening and knowing they will be okay. The circle keeps on spinning, growing stronger.

IT HAS BEEN proven in my life that when your prayers are about gratitude for what is already here, Creator and the universe ALWAYS send more. Always. When you pray for what you WANT, Creator and the universe only hear the wanting, and that's what you create—more wanting. Be thankful, offer prayers of gratitude for the blessings already in your life, whether health, prosperity or productivity, and more blessings will come.

TO RAISE THE sacred pipe of my being to Creator and Creation each morning is to bring myself into the full realization of my size and place. I belong. I am part of sacred energy, moving, spinning, growing, bringing everything into harmony. Without this sacred time of prayer and meditation, I am less able to do the work of each day—to reach out with empathy, compassion.

The miracle IS THAT WE ARE
HERE AT ALL

THE MIRACLE IS that we are here at all. Life itself is our greatest wonder. To simply BE is awe-inspiring. I believe this. Just as I believe it's pointless to waste time chasing after meaningless shit like fame and wealth and status. Better to spend time creating—good words, good feelings, good relationships, good memories—the grandest, most triumphant stories of our individual and collective time here. Creating those stories is a sacred act, and all that we are really meant to do. So don't look for me on the hilltop shouting. That's me in the valley with my hands in the dirt...

TO BE HERE
IS TO BE AFFECTED,
made more

THERE IS SUNLIGHT in the mountains today. The morning is crisp and clear as untrammelled thought. Against the sky, the trees raise crooked fingers in praise. To be here is to be affected, made more. Filled. The creative energy of the universe. Drink it in, my friends...

I WALK WITH the scars of a lifetime of living. Some were self-inflicted wounds. Some were caused by others. Either way, they mark the trajectory of six decades of experience with the ins and outs, ups and downs, doubts and certainties of my relationship with living. They mark the territory of my being. I don't regret a single one of them now. In fact, I'm thankful for them. My scars have the strange ability to remind me that my past was real, and what is real offers knowledge, understanding and an ultimate forgiveness.

HOME IS THE culmination of my hopes and dreams and desires. Home is a feeling in the centre of my chest of rightness, balance and harmony of the mind, body and spirit. Home is where the channel to Creator and the Grandmothers gets opened every day and where life gains its focal point. To be away from it, even for a day, is that acute awareness. It is also knowing that home is what I bring to it, and in that is the sure and quiet knowledge that home is within me and always was.

THE LOONS HAVE RETURNED. Their nattering is wonderful to hear and the loose wobble of their call in the darkness cheers me. Relatives. Always glad to see them when they return to visit.

POWWOW IS ABOUT celebrating the power of the earth. To dance is to bless it with each step. To sing is to honour it with each vocable, each sound I make.

LOVE IS NOT always the perfection of moments or the sum of all the shining days—sometimes it's to drift apart, to be broken, to be disassembled by life and living, but always to come back together and be each other's glue again. Love is an act of life, and we are made more by the living.

IT USED TO be that I knew the price of everything and the value of nothing. I was young then. Now, older, I'm thankful that's changed. These days, I know that the price of friendship is honesty and vulnerability, and friendship's value is priceless. I know that the price of belonging is humility and grace, and belonging's value is irreplaceable. I know that the price of love is equality and respect, and love's value is life-altering. Most of all, I know that the price of faith is the courage to walk through anything with belief in immaculate love—and the value of faith is eternal.

I FIND POLITICAL strength through spiritual strength. Each day is a smudge and a prayer of gratitude for everything, even the conflicts, for they are my teachers. For those who do not understand me, hear me, empathize with the struggles of my people, I pray in gratitude for their well-being, their wholeheartedness, their clarity of mind and the full sweep of their emotions to be brought forward into their days, just as I pray in gratitude for my own. In this way, I find peace, because the truth is that we are one body moving through time together.

SAGE, CEDAR, SWEET GRASS, tobacco. The sacred medicines. When you start your day with them, along with a prayer of gratitude, your energy becomes joined with the creative energy of the universe—and you may become a creator yourself if you choose and allow. That's the power of medicine.

WHAT DEFINES ME is not what I do but what I receive. Out of a deep spiritual yearning, I have received sobriety, recovery, and a working relationship with a god of my understanding—so that I have received grace. Out of that same yearning, I have received community, belonging, home and the opportunity to be productive—so that I have received prosperity. Spiritual yearning has brought me friends, fellowship, brotherhood, family and a life partner who expands me—so that I have received love. That same yearning has brought me calm, peace, prayer, compassion and forgiveness—so that I have received joy and freedom. What defines me is not what I do but what I receive, and I have received in great measure.

MISSING SOMEONE IS feeling a piece of your heart gone astray. Sure, it keeps beating, and sure, you keep breathing, but there's a gap in the rhythm of it, and in the rhythm of the everyday things around you. You seem to move a little less gracefully. But you still move, and that's the critical thing. Because missing someone doesn't mean things grind to a halt. Instead, it means you move out of gratitude for the gift of their presence in your life. You move to keep experiencing, to keep confronting life head-on, so that your return allows you to reunite with them as more human, more alive, more real.

missing
someone
IS FEELING
A PIECE OF YOUR
heart
gone
astray.

ME: I miss my mother sometimes. Really bad.

OLD WOMAN: Maybe try missing her really well.

ME: How do I do that?

OLD WOMAN: See that sunrise? See how beautiful the colours are? How clear and clean the air feels? How good it feels inside of you?

ME: Yes. It's wonderful.

OLD WOMAN: She lives in that. So maybe just say, "Thanks, Mom" when you see and feel things like that.

***

I miss my mother really well now.

VII.

joy

ALL WE HAVE
are moments

I WANT TO be unruly, live without rules. Not all of them—just the ones that restrain my curiosity, emotionality, spirituality, actuality and ability to be my authentic self. The ones that say, "Don't think, don't talk, don't feel." The ones that reduce me. The ones that tell me what a man should be. The ones that keep me chained to false narratives. I want to be unruly—to live beyond the NO and reside instead where everyone says, "Fuck, yeah!" to life and living.

ALL WE HAVE are moments. So live them as though not one can be wasted. Inhabit them, fill them with the light of your best good intention, honour them with your full presence, find the joy, the calm, the assuredness that allows the hours and the days to take care of themselves. If we can do that, we will have lived.

A MEMORY: I'M standing on a high shelf of ridge miles out in the wilderness, far from any hiking trail. There's a lake far below me. The sky is so blue I ache for it. I close my eyes and raise my head and face and arms to the sky. Everything is so keenly alive I'm lost in the thrall of it. When I open my eyes, there's another man thirty feet away lost in the same manner. We see each other. We smile. We laugh. We turn wordlessly and continue on our separate ways. The teaching? When we see each other through eyes of wonder, all barriers, all differences disappear. We are alive. We are joined. We are everything.

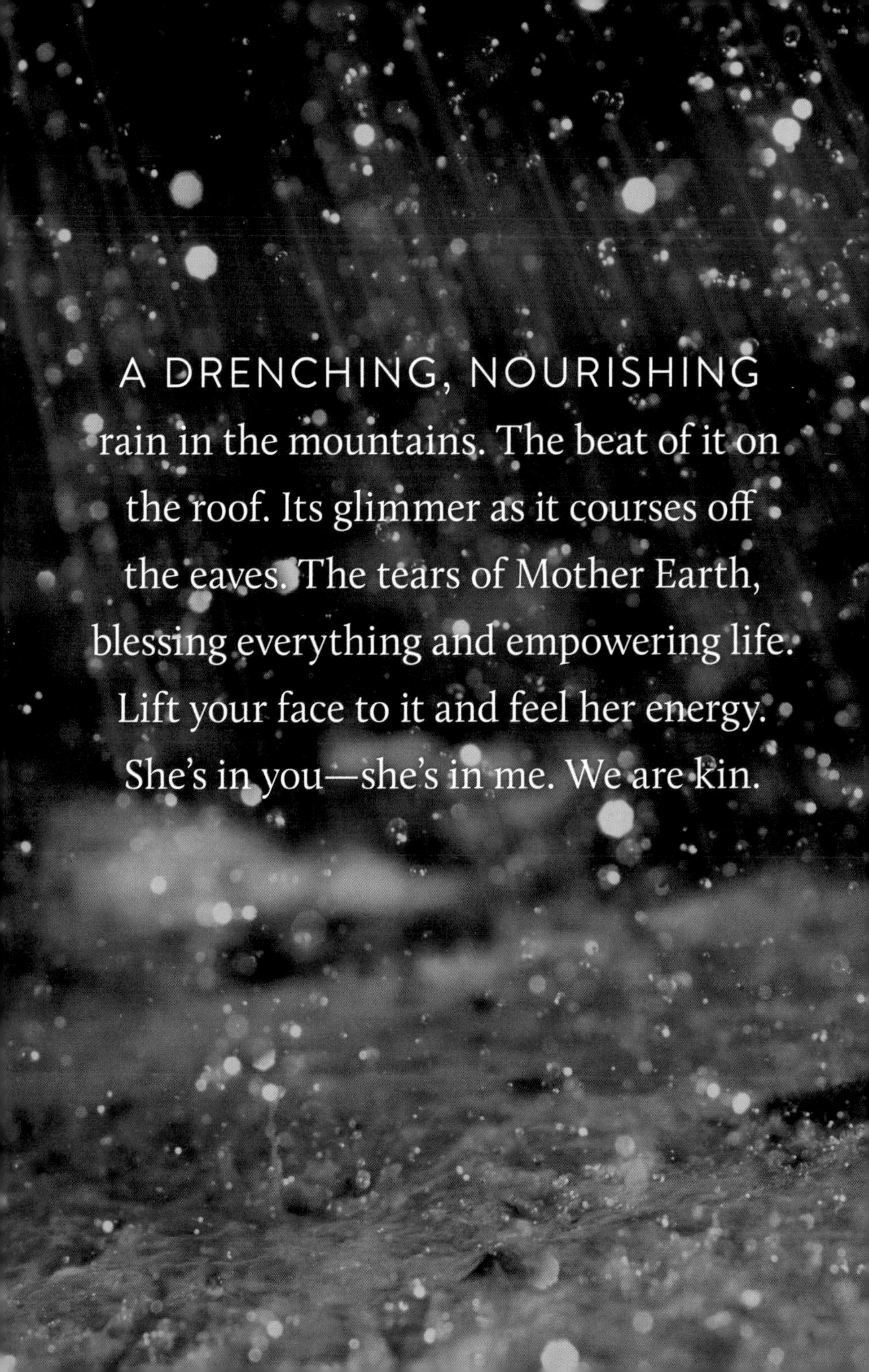

A DRENCHING, NOURISHING rain in the mountains. The beat of it on the roof. Its glimmer as it courses off the eaves. The tears of Mother Earth, blessing everything and empowering life. Lift your face to it and feel her energy. She's in you—she's in me. We are kin.

THE JOY IN HAVING SOMEONE special in your life isn't that they love the same things you do. The joy lies in knowing they love it that you love something.

I'M NOT HERE in this life to be well balanced or admired. I'm here to be an oddball, eccentric, different, wildly imaginative, creative, daring, curious, inventive and even a tad strange at times. I'm here to pray and chant and meditate and sing and find Creator in a blues riff, a sunrise, a touch or the laughter of children. I'm here to discover ME in all of that. I'm here to add clunky, chunky and funky bits of me to the swirl and swagger and churn of life and living. It demands I be authentic. So when you look out at the world, that's me dancing in the fields...

"HOME IS A truth you carry inside you." I wrote that a few years back, and I still believe it. Out on the porch, with coffee, a breeze and the calming scent of sacred medicines in my hair, I sit in my truth—this building, this relationship, this day, this certain and assured contact with Creator. I am home. Not just on this street but in this body, on this planet, in this universe.

THIS IS CREATOR'S fire, this match that flares. This is Creator's medicine that curls, plumes and rises with the touch of flame. This is Creator's morning, the light spreading outward, easing shadow to rest. This is Creator's world, this pure and perfect Creation. And as the smoke rises, my mind empties, my heart opens, my spirit soars, and the prayer I offer allows this morning energy to enter me. I am become it—and it becomes me. I am alive.

my mind
EMPTIES,
my heart
OPENS,
my spirit
SOARS

DON'T JUST WRITE what you know. Write what you wish to know. What you reveal to yourself, you reveal to the reader. Storytelling is about discovery.

AS LONG AS poems conserve the language of old ecstasies, there is hope for art. As long as twice-told tales ring with the clarity of blunt truths or wild, knee-slapping humour, there is hope for art. As long as lines curve beyond the linear scope of our thinking and lead the eye to recognize what it has never seen before, there is hope for art. Write, then. Paint. Sing. Act. Play. Raise through art the gamut of our collective humanity, our burgeoning spirit, so that Creator might see Herself in everything and smile.

STANDING IN THE early morning chill, clearing the car of snow, scraping ice from the windows, I look up and around me at a morning filled with things to see: the way the ice fog magnifies the mountain in the near distance so that it appears closer, the ballet of cat tracks in the snow, the bare trees like arterial networks in the dimness, the house slumped like a great sleeping bear under the white rug of winter. It occurs to me that the secret of fully being here, walking the skin of this planet, is to learn to see things as though I were looking at them for the first time, or the last. Nothing is too small then, too mundane, too usual. Everything is wonder. Everything is magical. Everything moves my spirit...and I am spiritual.

Everything
MOVES MY SPIRIT.

TO TELL. TO use the act of breathing to shape air into sounds that take on the context of language that lifts and transports those who hear it, takes them beyond what they think and know and feel and empowers them to think and feel and know even more. We're all storytellers, really. That's what we do. That is our power as human beings. Not to tell people how to think and feel and therefore know—but through our stories allow them to discover questions within themselves. Turn off your TV and your devices and talk to each other. Share stories. Be joined, transported and transformed.

DANCE,
dang it,
THAT'S WHAT
FEET
ARE FOR!

Acknowledgements

WE CARRY THE embers of all the things that burned and raged in us. Pains and sorrows, to be sure, but also triumphs, joys, victories and moments of clear-eyed vision. People give us those. People cause flames to rise in our hearts and minds and spirits, and life would not be life without them. My journey has been blessed by folks who stuck around until the miracle happened and I could begin to become the person I was created to be. This book would not have happened without the influence and help of so many.

Especially: Shelagh Rogers, my Chosen Sister and inspiring light for twenty-five years now, love is such a small word when I think of you. Joseph Boyden, my fellow scribe and brother who accepts me warts and all: I love you, too, my brother. Nick Pitt, a tremendous friend who has stood beside me when others would have fled. Rodger W. Ross, another great friend and brother for thirty-six years now, even when we were apart. Mista Wasis (Greg Dreaver), my enduring example of "warrior." Tantoo Cardinal, my Cree sister, who has always led me by her shining example: a great, great lady.

I'd be remiss if I didn't mention: Dan Ferguson, my brother in the journey, who has taught me so much about becoming a good man. My Sunday breakfast brothers, Yves M., Everett S., Don M., Melvin T. and Kenny B., you guys are my anchor and the ones I turn to for the vision of who I want to be when I grow up. My sisters in the journey, Julie T., Jessica D., Betty G., Lisa F., Rosie H., Sharon M. and Flora K., thank you all for inspiring me to move gently among you.

My ceremonial family, Sherri Chisan, Vincent Steinhauer, Kevin Knight, Rick Turner, Rick Two Feathers, Chris Morrison, Greg Eustache, Dave Manuel, Keith Matthew, Quinton W. Crow Shoe, Reg Crow Shoe and James Makokis: thank you for sharing the teachings and the way.

Daniela Ginta and Max, Hilary Chambers, Dawn Maracle, Stewart Duncan, Tom Gilbert, Mike and Kate Gilgan, Dean Gladue, Elizabeth Gray, Andy Jones, Peter and Nancy Mutrie, Doug Perry, Crystal Shawanda, Teneil Whiskeyjack, Michelle Thrush, Waubgeshig Rice: you have all added so much to the fabric and texture of this life.

My agents, John Pearce and Chris Casuccio, for the enduring loyalty; all the folks at Westwood Creative Artists; Barbara Pulling for her editorial genius; all the folks at Douglas & McIntyre and Harbour Publishing; my national speaking rep, Christine Brown, at Keynote Speakers Canada for getting these meditations—

and me—out to so many groups, organizations and communities; and the organizer of my life, Lisa Lalonde, for keeping my ducks in a row and making sure I eat right on the road.

There are so many more. I didn't forget you; I just ran out of room. I am so blessed to have all of you in my life! You know who you are...

PHOTO CREDITS: p.2 hegadex.com/AdobeStock; p.4 iStock.com/Robert Koopmans; p.6 iStock.com/Veronica Bogaerts; p.8 R_Koopmans/iStock/Thinkstock; p.10 Tom Thulen/Alamy Stock Photo; p.14 Vadven/iStock/Thinkstock; p.17 iStock.com/robertnowland; p.18 Richard Wagamese; p.22 Picture-Project/iStock/Thinkstock; p.24 Hemera Technologies/AbleStock.com/Thinkstock; p.27 Richard Wagamese; p.28 Ulzanna/iStock/Thinkstock; p.31 Comstock/Stockbyte/Thinkstock; p.34 Vadven/iStock/Thinkstock; p.37 hinzundkunz/iStock/Thinkstock; p.41 iStock.com/PaulReevesPhotography; p.42 Apriori1/iStock/Thinkstock; p.45 MinoruFuruse/iStock/Thinkstock; p.47 ChristiLaLiberte/iStock/Thinkstock; p.48 Mark Windom/Stocksy United; p.50 kelifamily/AdobeStock; p.54 Jupiterimages/PHOTOS.com/Thinkstock; p.56 Francis Vachon/Alamy Stock Photo; p.58 Medio-images/Photodisc/Thinkstock; p.62 Simone Rochon/Stocksy United; p.65 RasikaSekhara/iStock/Thinkstock; p.69 Jacqui Miller/Stocksy United; p.73 Richard Wagamese; p.77 MasaoTaira/iStock/Thinkstock; p.79 Cherish Bryck/Stocksy United; p.80 OlgaPink/iStock/Thinkstock; p.84 Luke Gram/Stocksy United; p.87 Wirepec/iStock/Thinkstock; p.88 Cory Stevens/iStock/Thinkstock; p.91 iStock.com/Robert Koopmans; p.92 nattaponsukjit/iStock/Thinkstock; p.95 iStock.com/ImagineGolf; p.96 underworld111/iStock/Thinkstock; p.99 valleyboi63/iStock/Thinkstock; p.100 Michael Overbeck/Stocksy United; p.103 Nateskee/iStock/Thinkstock; p.105 Rastan/iStock/Thinkstock; p.106 maksime/iStock/Thinkstock; p.109 Guoqiang Xue/Alamy Stock Photo; p.112 tortoon/iStock/Thinkstock; p.116 Michael Overbeck/Stocksy United; p.119 studio-laska/iStock/Thinkstock; p.123 iStock.com/Ben Grace; p.124 iStock.com/Robert Koopmans; p.128 snowflock/iStock/Thinkstock; p.133 Luke Gram/Stocksy United; p.136 videnovic/iStock/Thinkstock; p.138 Hemera Technologies/PHOTOS.com/Thinkstock; p.141 Ruslan Nassyrov/Hemera/Thinkstock; p.144 ch__ch/iStock/Thinkstock; p.146 Design Pics/Thinkstock; p.149 Renald Bourque/iStock/Thinkstock; p.150 Paul Edmondson/Stocksy United; p.154 KarelGallas/iStock/Thinkstock; p.157 sansa55/iStock/Thinkstock; p.160 Yvette Lehmann; p.163 David De Lossy/Photodisc/Thinkstock; p.164 Richard Wagamese; p.167 VBaleha/iStock/Thinkstock; p.168 Todd Mintz / Alamy Stock Photo; p.171 Luke Gram/Stocksy United; p.173 Real-WorldPhoto/Alamy Stock Photo